Meeting Children's Emotional Needs

PRENTICE-HALL PSYCHOLOGY SERIES

Arthur T. Jersild, *Editor*

KATHERINE E. D'EVELYN

Chief Psychologist and Coordinator
Psychological Services
Great Neck Public Schools
Great Neck, New York

A
GUIDE
FOR
TEACHERS

Meeting Children's Emotional Needs

PRENTICE-HALL, INC. . *Englewood Cliffs, N. J.*

Library of Congress
Catalog Card No.: 57-9388

First printing .... April, 1957
Second printing .... September, 1957
Third printing .... January, 1958
Fourth printing .... July, 1958
Fifth printing .... January, 1959

PRINTED IN THE UNITED STATES OF AMERICA
57424

Preface

Teachers may need some constructive assistance in meeting the emotional needs of children in the classroom. How the school can help meet these needs is discussed in the first part of this text. The second section presents specific cases of disturbed children and suggests ways of dealing with their problems. The necessity for cooperation between school and home is stressed in the final part. By emphasizing the interrelationship of good mental health and learning, this book points out the importance of emotional well-being in the educational process.

Attention is given to the school's responsibility for providing teachers with the advice and services of a psychologist. Case histories are cited to illustrate symptoms of emotional disturbance and to describe ways of helping children by means of school and community resources. Most teachers will find similar adjustment problems in their own classrooms.

I have worked with children for many years, first as a classroom teacher, then as a psychologist. From this experience I have tried to present information and ideas that will help teachers in their challenging, important, and sometimes discouraging task. The rewards of this profession are self-evident, and it is hoped that *Meeting Children's Emotional Needs* will encourage its readers to continue with renewed energy and with the strengthened conviction that the teacher's function is a significant and vital one.

Were this book dedicated, it would be to the many fine teachers whose work inspired me to undertake this writing. I wish to express my deep appreciation to Mrs. Alice Lofblad and Mrs. Gretchen Dolliff for their editorial suggestions and for their assistance in typing much of the manuscript. I am also grateful to other friends whose comments were of such great help.

KATHERINE E. D'EVELYN

Contents

THE CLASSROOM AND MENTAL HEALTH

Part Two

SPECIALIZED NEEDS
OF INDIVIDUAL CHILDREN

Part Three

HOW THE TEACHER WORKS WITH PARENTS AND THE SCHOOL PSYCHOLOGIST

Meeting
Children's
Emotional
Needs

Part One

The classroom and mental health

1

Introduction

Only when their emotional needs are met can children learn and work out their relationships with others. Teachers have always met the emotional needs of children; this is nothing new. It is what I call the *more than teaching* that they have always done, either consciously or unconsciously. The teacher who meets the emotional needs of his pupils is aware of the relationship between emotions and learning, between emotions and mental health. Conscious of these facts,

3

this teacher tries to preserve an attitude toward the children coming to him that will enable those with good mental health to maintain it and those with poor mental health to be benefited. This task can be difficult, especially when there are several disturbed children in a group. Ordinarily, the teacher who is aware of children's needs, who has some insight into their behavior, as well as into his own, can do a remarkably fine job of helping them develop intellectual skills and good interpersonal relationships concomitantly.

. These statements are not designed to make teachers feel unduly burdened or to arouse guilty feelings over some children they may have been concerned about in the past. Rather, they are made to give credit where credit is due, to encourage the many teachers who are doing a fine job of meeting emotional needs in the classroom, and to alert other teachers to the possibilities open to them.

As the discussion moves along in this book, it is hoped that teachers will also realize that there are children they may not be able to help learn adequately or gain good mental health. While they will regret this, they should not feel guilty or blame themselves. If they will learn to recognize symptoms indicating serious emotional disturbance, they can seek help for these disturbed children from community resources or through the school psychologist. Many teachers blame themselves for their children's failures and problems unjustly; many teachers do not seek help when they should.

In a statement above, developing intellectual skills and fostering good interpersonal relationships were linked together as though part of the same process and interdependent. Unfortunately, this is not true in all instances, for some children adopt neurotic behavior patterns where a one-sided development takes place. It is true, however, that for most children, learning and satisfactory interpersonal relationships take place in conjunction. Before discussing special adjustment problems, it is well to get a picture of normal behavior and normal emotional needs. By doing this, it is easier to understand deviant behavior.

Also, in a previous statement, the term *more than teaching* was used. Perhaps this sounds vague, but later discussions will elaborate and clarify its meaning.

Meeting the emotional needs of children does not imply that the teacher carries out therapy, and is, therefore, a therapist. I believe that therapy should be undertaken only by a well-trained person — a social worker, a psychologist, or a psychiatrist. The teacher cannot, and should not, give therapy in the classroom; he does not have the proper training and the classroom is not the place for such treatment.

If the teacher maintains an atmosphere conducive to good mental health, however, the classroom can have a therapeutic effect on the child. The teacher has a very real function to perform in meeting the emotional needs of children, and this function should not be confused with or impaired by misdirected attempts at therapy.

The next three chapters discuss what is entailed in maintaining an atmosphere conducive to good mental health. Since each stage of development is built upon the previous one, it is essential to follow the sequential development of emotional needs by reading the three chapters in their given order.

2

Emotional Needs of the Young Child

A good school provides much to meet the emotional needs of its children. The curriculum, the teacher, and the other children are all important factors in the child's emotional and intellectual development. The school's contribution varies according to the age and developmental level of the child. While a certain child's needs may, and often do, differ from those of other children the same age, the average teacher can discover the needs common within a certain age span. This awareness must not shut his eyes to the requirements of particular individuals in the group; he should try to meet the emotional needs of the group *and* the individual. Good teachers have always done this, often without stopping to analyze their procedures. What they did seemed "right" for a particular child.

School encompasses a wide span in the life of a child — from five to sixteen, seventeen, or eighteen in most public schools. Beginning with the kindergarten level, a description of the normal child's emotional needs will be given, together with suggestions as to how they can be met by the teacher.

When a child comes to school at five or six, he needs acceptance and much support in many ways from his teacher. This support and acceptance can be partially given by individual notice and attention through a smile, a pat on the shoulder, or an attentive ear to what the child has to say. Tactful praise can be helpful if given for the individual himself, not praise for competing with the group. It does not help a child emotionally to make him feel he is better than his classmates. Praise best can be given through a smile of recognition for some accomplishment or by a sincere, "Well done." If a child is commended in competition with the group — "Yours is the best drawing," or "Yours is the best behavior," or "I wish the others could do as well," — both he and the other children will feel that the teacher likes them only when they achieve in a certain way or behave in a certain fashion. Some children never can achieve or behave in the "approved" fashion, and they thus feel like outcasts whenever they hear other children receive this sort of praise.

While children learn through approval and while praise is one way of giving them support, the emotional effects of competitive praise as described above cannot be anything but harmful. For healthy emotional development, little children need to feel that the teacher accepts them for themselves and not alone for their good behavior and accomplishments. Also, it is hard for a small child accustomed to the comparatively sheltered home environment, where he gets considerable attention and support from an adult, to become one of a large group of children in which he is relatively unnoticed. He needs as much constructive individual attention and acceptance from the teacher as he can get, but it should not be emphasized — through the kind of competitive praise or attention described above — that he is competing for the individual acceptance which he needs for emotional survival and well-being.

When the teacher is able through his accepting, kindly manner to make young children feel that he likes them, will protect them, will treat them with dignity and respect, they expand in this new environment and take steps toward the greater independence, development of new skills, and acceptance of other people that most children of this age are ready for. Acceptance of other people is an important step in emotional development and mental health.

Unless the child feels accepted and emotionally secure in the school environment, unless he gets the attention and support he needs from the teacher, he will not learn what we expect him to learn, nor will he make what we call in pedagogic language "a good social adjustment." There are some children who do not thrive even though the teacher gives them the necessary emotional security. These children will be discussed later when special guidance problems are explored.

Another mental health or emotional need of the young child is the feeling of accomplishment and the inner strength that comes with accomplishment. Some writers have called this a *feeling of adequacy*. It becomes the teacher's task to see that children gain a sense of accomplishment. Part of the something that goes on "over and above teaching" is the teacher's awareness of this need and his ability to implement it. He will not insist that all children learn to read and write at the same time because he knows that to do so would cause some children to fail. If they fail at these teacher-imposed tasks, they do not gain this feeling of accomplishment and inner strength. If they are not ready to learn to read and write, the teacher should give them other things to do that will help them feel that they, too, are learning and growing. This is important because they see *other* children "learning" and because their parents expect *them* "to learn." Most teachers of today have become adept at planning a constructive program for young children. Thus, individual differences in readiness for learning are considered, and the children's needs are satisfied.

It is, perhaps, best that a certain point be made clear at this time. To say that young children need a sense of accomplishment for intellectual and emotional growth does not mean that they should never experience failure. It is unrealistic to assume that no one should experience failure. Small children can learn from failure if certain conditions are present. They must have the interest, the motivation, the skill, the intellectual and emotional readiness for a certain task. If these conditions are present, they can and do learn from failure. Given a teacher-imposed task before success is possible, however, the child can learn only one thing from failure — that he has failed. In repeated failure, he loses teacher and parent approval, and even equally important, the feeling of inner strength.

Schools unwittingly foster mental illness and maladjustment when they fail in this important function, that of helping the young child to gain a feeling of *accomplishment*. It is through this feeling that self-confidence is born, and self-confidence is one of the roots of good mental health. In most maladjustments and mental ills, the lack of self-confidence and its concomitant feeling of worthlessness are present.

The young child can gain a feeling of accomplishment from many sources, and the teacher should be on the lookout for such sources and foster them. It may be through the arts, through dramatic play, through academic skills, through ability to tell stories, ride a bicycle, or play marbles.

Part of the teacher's function in this process is to gain the parent's assistance, especially if the teacher is fostering self-confidence in the child through some source the parent might not understand. Parents frequently see the importance of academic achievement alone for children six and seven years of age, and need the help of the teacher to realize that self-confidence gained in any one area carries over into all other areas, too.

Because the young child is so dependent upon the teacher for support and acceptance, he, like the parent, must know how to give the needed support and, at the same time, how to let or encourage the child to become more independent. Most teachers have definite ideas about how independent children of specific ages should be. These ideas are based partly on experience and partly on information gleaned from courses in child development. Certainly it is true that we expect the child of five, six, or seven to become progressively independent and less in need of teacher support, direction, and control. Most children like the satisfaction of growing independence as long as they do not feel pushed, confused, or rejected by the teacher. The latter can tell how a child feels by the reaction to his expectation for more independence. If the child responds successfully and happily to added independence, the teacher knows that he is ready for it, whether it be more freedom of choice, less direction in a given task, or less supervision in play and work activities. If the child responds with confusion, whining, tears, quarreling, disorganized behavior, or passive inactivity, the teacher knows that he still needs active support.

No child can be *forced* into independent action successfully from the standpoint of emotional well-being. He must be *led* gradually into it as he begins to feel more comfortable in the particular situation, when he gains confidence in his ability to handle the situation, and when he considers the teacher is to be trusted in giving him any needed help without scolding or disapproval.

The teacher's part in guiding children into more independence, then, is to watch for the signs mentioned above and to plan accordingly. He need not hesitate to give more support than he thinks a child should have, for it is the secure and confident child who moves forward, not the child who is pushed before he is ready. One of the teacher's biggest problems with young children is in relation to this whole matter of giving *enough* and the *right kind* of support *when* it is needed. Young children are still in the process of building controls and feel safer when the teacher gives them the necessary help to maintain control.

For example, the young child is largely a creature of emotion; his feelings, desires, and wishes are strong and primitive. He naturally wishes to satisfy his desires, and his efforts are bent toward feeling comfortable and happy. By the time the child of five comes to school, he has learned that certain of his actions bring adult approval, while certain others bring disapproval. This is inevitable because we live in a particular culture in which it is the job of adults to acquaint children with the customary social patterns. If the child's earlier experiences are with loving, helpful parents, it becomes important to him to have their approval. He curbs certain feelings and desires, and tempers certain actions to gain their approval. He does this because he is dependent upon his parents for his existence, and their approval is, therefore, necessary and all-important to him.

But it is not easy to give up one's own strong and primitive wishes, and so it takes time for the child to build controls sufficiently strong to enable him to do without this adult support. It is, therefore, unrealistic for teachers of young children to expect them to take full responsibility for their own planning and behavior. The children may wish to do so because the teacher wishes them to, but if their behavior becomes quarrelsome, chaotic, and disorganized, the teacher must realize that they are not ready for so much responsibility.

When children lose self-control they become confused and feel guilty. They are afraid of their own wild, disorganized, aggressive behavior, and are relieved when the teacher helps them to restore order and an atmosphere of comfortable goodwill. This does not mean that the teacher should give the children no part in planning or that he should not let them have as much freedom and self-control as they can handle. It merely means that he gives them the *kindly support* and *sets the limits* they need in maintaining good inter-group relationships in work and play. This requires skill and an understanding of children's reactions and needs.

Because adults must be, in a certain measure, restrictive and prohibitive with children as they help them understand cultural expectations, children are frustrated in the expressions of some of their wishes and feelings. In all children, this necessary frustration — even though slight — arouses some feelings of resentment toward adults. Since it is not safe to show this resentment toward the powerful and necessary adults, it is directed toward safer individuals — usually peers. This explains much friction and quarreling among children.

In our middle-class culture, we try early to curb children's excessive aggressive acts toward others. Children become, therefore, frustrated, but are not permitted to express their resentment. It is hard for many children to build controls strong enough to prevent the spilling over of these repressed emotions in disorganized behavior. Because the child has been made to feel that such behavior is unacceptable, he feels guilty when he loses control. When he feels guilty, he usually becomes anxious. Anxiety makes for less control, and so we have a vicious circle.

Perceiving these circumstances, the teacher who is concerned with the child's emotional needs helps the child maintain control, and behave acceptably. This is a good mental health practice, and can be accomplished without the teacher's being repressively dictatorial or harsh. The child welcomes firm control from a loving, accepting adult — teacher or parent. He feels safer, and since he feels safer, he can expand into learning and broader interpersonal experiences with his peers.

In the process of building controls, some young children who are struggling with this process show a particular behavior that teachers find disturbing. This behavior is that of "telling on" other children. Many teachers believe the tattletale is to be reproved or scolded. They do not see that in the young child this behavior is a step in building controls. The child who tattles would like to be taking part in the forbidden activity, but he has taken a step forward in control. He does not participate, but since the temptation is so great, he comes to the teacher for help. By telling the teacher, he is seeking his approval for not participating and thus gains strength to resist. Most children do not need this approval very long, and if the teacher merely commends him for not taking part in the forbidden act, he gains further strength so that in time he no longer needs his support in resisting this particular temptation. He has built his own inner control.

If tattling behavior persists to any great extent in a child beyond the third grade, the teacher should recognize this as a sign that the child has not established good peer relationships, and should be concerned. Somewhere between eight and nine years of age, children reach the stage of emotional and social development at which they form a strong identification with their own age mates. It is the beginning of group loyalty, and is a step — an important step forward — in emotional development and good mental health. It means that the child is becoming less dependent upon the adult, although he still needs considerable support; he is beginning to see his classmates as individuals like himself whom he can sympathize with, love, and unite with against repressive adults.

This identification with peers has two significant psychological meanings: the child is taking one of the necessary steps toward emotional weaning from the parents in the process of growing into an independent and self-sufficient adult, and he is accepting and being accepted by his contemporaries. His peers are the people he will live and work with, and unless he can accept and be accepted by them, he is not making adequate emotional growth or maintaining good mental health. The teacher's function in connection with this process is to be aware of this important step in development; to encourage budding friendships through classroom seating, grouping, and work assignments; to encourage parents to make it easier for children to visit and play with each other after school, if the community is one where distances and transportation are a problem.

Teachers and parents who are aware of this stage of development often become concerned over the child's choice of friends. At this age, friendships are fluid, and it is good for the child to experiment. If one child takes a completely passive role in the friendship, he may in time, and with opportunity, find another friend with whom he can establish a more balanced relationship. It is best not to show concern over friendships. But, in realizing the child's limited experience, the parent and teacher can open other opportunities for further friendships to be formed. Usually, unless a friendship is mutually satisfiying, it will not be of long duration. The important point is that the child is beginning to accept and be accepted in a peer relationship by his classmates. It is the beginning that will blossom and strengthen as the child progresses through school.

We cannot leave this brief discussion of the young child's emotional needs without mentioning another important one. This is his need for freedom to be creative, in thought and in deed. The teacher who permits creative thinking by respecting the child's thoughts, suggestions, and contributions is laying the groundwork for future creative, independent thought. No individual can be truly emotionally healthy who does not have this power of creative thinking fostered and who does not feel that his thoughts are worthy of consideration. The young child, to be sure, will proceed haltingly and may not be very successful. Unless a start is made, however, he will become a person who depends upon others to do his thinking for him. Creative thinking is meant here to include both problem solving and expression of esthetic feelings. This creativity can be fostered by accepting suggestions, ideas, and thoughts without ridicule and without making the child self-conscious through amazed comment or praise. Some adults tend to make the young child self-conscious and precocious by exploiting creative deeds or expressions through calling upon the child to "show-off" to others. This practice spoils true creativity in the young child.

Creativity in deed is equally important. As a rule, the young child will be creative if he is not repressed, if he is given materials to work with that lend themselves to creativity, and if he is not made afraid by adult criticism. Any non-static material can stimulate the young child's expression — paints; clay; crayons; paper, scissors, and paste; ribbons and bits of brightly colored cloth; simple musical instruments of all kinds, especially simple percussion instruments; blocks; and sand. Given materials to use and a permissive atmosphere in which to work, children expand and experiment. The adult does not direct, but can help by introducing new materials and new ideas to stimulate the child's imagination and widen his interests; this is necessary and good. Without adult assistance in bringing in new materials and in widening interests, the child does not move forward as he should or could.

There is a fine balance here between superimposing adult ideas of creative art, music, and expression upon children and in opening doors to freedom of self-expression. Unless the teacher has a genuine respect for what the child creates and understands its possible meaning to him as "his work," he is in danger of imposing his own standards or of stifling the first hesitating ventures of young children who feel that without adult approval they dare not venture forth. The important point to keep in mind is the meaning of all creative action to the developing personality. The child who is not afraid to be creative is the child who is free, spontaneous, and self-confident. All of these qualities are relative in degree in each person, and all are the result of ability plus experience and interpersonal relationships. The teacher can foster the roots of these qualities which have been implanted in the earliest years of life during the interpersonal, experiential living in the home prior to attending school. If the child's personality has been warped before coming to school, it will be difficult for the teacher to reawaken or to reeducate the natural desire for creative action. If the roots are already there, it is easier to help them develop further.

Thus, the end results of the child's creative acts are not as important as their significance in regard to his emotional health and intellectual development. The child who is creative in thought and deed is on the road to sound emotional health and successful intellectual development. Creativity connotes constructive thinking and functioning, and is basic to learning and mental health. If the young child is not creative, we must look for something repressive in his past interpersonal relationships. To help him, we need to be warmly accepting of him as a person and patiently encouraging to his feeble, beginning steps to create.

There is one other aspect of creative expression through all forms of art media which should be mentioned: the free use of art media can also be emotionally beneficial in serving as a tension reducer. Everyone needs tension reducers, especially children who are under adult supervision and restriction much of the time. Anger and resentment, as well as exuberant good feelings, can be expressed in a satisfying way to act as a safety valve when feelings are explosive or when there is a desire to put happy feelings into some permanent form of expression. To young children, expression through art media or music is as natural as expression through speech. They would all use these forms of expression if given the opportunity and the freedom to do so. If they are restricted at home because of lack of materials, rules as to cleanliness and quiet, or adult criticism, and if this process is continued later at school, these forms of expression are killed in all but the most gifted and strongly motivated. When the creative drive is killed, beneficial mental health activities are lost, and the child never develops his full capacities.

Since the young child is very much the creature of his environment, vastly influenced by the adults in his environment, it is essential that there be some unity, harmony, and consistency in approach and understanding between parents and teacher if the child is to maintain good mental health and have satisfactory learning experiences. The child looks to his parent and his teacher for acceptance and support, as well as guidance in developing standards and values. When the school tries to set standards and customs foreign to the child's home, when the teacher fails to understand the cultural life of the home and inadvertently or unthinkingly criticizes or ridicules certain customs or expressions, certain manners or lack of manners, the young child becomes confused. If he comes to love his teacher, he is torn in his loyalties between teacher and parent. If he distrusts the teacher, he becomes suspicious of him and anything he wants to teach. He becomes unhappy and rebellious at school, or holds himself aloof from school activities and learning experiences.

If the parent, on the other hand, criticizes the school, the teacher, or the curriculum, the child is confused and distrustful; the same effect as described above ensues. Anything which undermines the child's affection and trust for either parent or teacher makes him insecure in his relationships with these adults and renders his life in both places unsatisfactory. Usually, the young child has placed trust in his parent before coming to school, so it is the school relationship that suffers when there is lack of unity between home and school.

Teachers of young children need to know their parents and their environmental influences so they will not needlessly cause them confusion, unhappiness, and emotional disturbance. Teachers and parents should know each other as interested partners in the process of helping the children feel secure in their acceptance of them, their home, and their school. Teachers need to gain the parents' understanding and support for what they are doing at school so that the parents can, in turn, give the child understanding and support when he talks about his school or brings home a school report or communication about some activity.

If the teacher is helping the child gain a feeling of accomplishment in reading or in any other activity and the parent thinks the child is not doing well, the child does not know whom to believe; his self-confidence is undermined. Teacher and parent need to know what is going on and to recognize the part each can play in developing the child's emotional well-being.

As a child grows older he can better accept some differences of opinion between his parent and teacher, especially if he feels secure and successful both at home and at school and does not let these differences upset him emotionally. But the young child is still too dependent upon adults to be able to understand or assimilate such disharmony with equanimity. The bedrock of his foundations is shaken, and he shows his emotional unhappiness in some kind of disturbed behavior if the home-school conflict persists.

SUMMARY

In summarizing the teacher's part in meeting the emotional needs of young children, it can be seen that he has a large and important contribution to make to the emotional and intellectual well-being of his charges.

The dependency needs of young children are such that unless they are met by the significant adults in their environment, they will not thrive emotionally or intellectually. Teachers, therefore, cannot overlook these needs in their work with young children.

Ways in which these dependency needs can be met have been discussed; also, the concomitant need for growing independence has been stressed.

Before a child goes to school he looks to the parent for support and praise. You hear him say, "My mother says . . ." or "My father says . . . ." After he has been in school for a time and feels loved and accepted by the teacher who helps him learn and succeed, he adds another person to this list and you hear him say, "My teacher says . . . ." The necessity for harmony and unity between home and school can, therefore, be seen. Since both parent and teacher are significant in his life, and since he has had very limited experience, he looks to them for strength, approval, and guidance. The consequences of serious, continuing conflict between parent and teacher, between home and school, are disturbing to the child's intellectual development and emotional well-being.

The teachers of young children have an especially important function to perform—one that is *over and above teaching*.

3

Emotional Needs of the Intermediate, Pre-adolescent Child

Some time between eight and nine years of age, the child passes gradually into a phase of his development which lasts throughout pre-adolescence. This stage is characterized by a number of behavorial changes. Any third grade teacher knows what these changes are, for although the changes come gradually and their degree varies from child to child, there is no mistaking them. The children become more independent and ask for less advice and reassurance from the teacher. They begin to show a group solidarity which ties in with growing peer identification and acceptance. If peer identification and teacher rapport are good, there is sustained group cooperation. If peer identification is good but teacher rapport poor, the child may become rebellious or defiant in behavior toward the teacher. Rebelliousness or defiance on the part of a younger child isolates him because the group is so completely dependent upon the teacher for approval and direction. On the part of the pre-adolescent, however, rebellion may strengthen his relationship with the group. This is because the group, as a whole, is beginning to need less adult approval and to feel strength in peer identification.

This development is fascinating to observe, and, of course, the ideal classroom situation is one in which both teacher-child rapport and peer rapport are good. It is ideal because the child of this age needs, for his emotional well-being, both teacher and peer acceptance and rapport. If peer acceptance is lacking, the child may withdraw completely from group activities, cling to the teacher for attention, bully the other children, or become a "tattletale." If teacher acceptance is lacking, the child may still gain group acceptance, unless his behavior is so defiant it upsets the harmony of the classroom; in this case his behavior disturbs the other children, who may then reject him. In losing teacher acceptance, the child feels rejected or repulsed. He still has great need for acceptance, although he will not show it in the way the younger child does. To summarize: in spite of his growing independence and unity with the group, the pre-adolescent needs continued affectional acceptance by the teacher in addition to peer acceptance for good mental health and emotional development.

The teacher shows acceptance of the pre-adolescent in much the same way that he shows it to the younger child: by kindly, affectionate interest in him; by respect for his ideas, suggestions, and group contributions; by helping him achieve success in his lessons; and by letting him become more independent. The pre-adolescent needs to feel that he is a liked member of the classroom "family" with an important place that only he can fill. Treating him as a person who warrants respect and consideration is one way of assuring him of this acceptance.

Desire and need for more independence is a normal stage in emotional growth, and recognition of this fact by the teacher fosters good mental health and becomes part of his acceptance of the child as a person. Understanding that these two needs—teacher acceptance and desire for independence —are present and may cause conflict in the child will enable the teacher to understand him and be more ready to tolerate minor rebelliousness or defiance. Some rebelliousness may come if the child feels he is being "treated like a baby," is not a person whose wishes and ideas are worthy of consideration, or is made to lose face with his peers by some word or deed of the adult. The rebellious child usually fears he has lost the teacher's acceptance, and he feels guilty about his defiance. When guilt is added to the already injured feelings of the defiant child, he is in an emotional state in which he needs the teacher's assistance to regain his status as a group member in good standing. The child needs to feel he has not lost the teacher's acceptance, even though his acts are disapproved; he needs to regain his self-respect, which has suffered in the emotional upheaval.

For most children, increasing independence is acquired with only minor rebelliousness. As a rule, continual defiance in the pre-adolescent indicates a previous lack of harmonious and satisfying relationships with parental figures in the home and school. Ways in which the teacher can help such a child will be discussed in another section of this book.

Because the pre-adolescent is usually interested in learning and desires to be successful in his school work, the teacher can show his acceptance by helping him—with patient good humor, if that is essential—to get him over a hump in some learning process. For most of these children, school has become a large and important part of life, just as business and homemaking are to their parents. In school they are part of a peer culture which has become extremely significant to them. Since school is such a large part of their lives, the success they achieve there becomes a potent force in their mental health. Being successful in school means to the child what success in a profession or a job does to the adult. He gains a feeling of inner power and ability to master situations; without this confidence, he loses the courage and the initiative necessary to stand up to life. No child can face daily failure and the subsequent loss of adult, peer, and self approval without emotional crippling that may lead to delinquency or emotional illness. One of the greatest challenges to teachers is helping all children feel successful. Of course, this is not always possible, but probably much more could be done in schools than is being attempted now. This subject will be discussed further when cases are described of children who fail.

The pre-adolescent, as well as the young child, needs to have tasks he is capable of meeting with success. The teacher plays a vital role in making *all* school experiences as successful and constructive as possible. *All* school experiences here refers to both learning and interpersonal ones. The pre-adolescent who is drawn into the on-going life of an interesting classroom and guided and supported by an affectionate, firm, and good-humored teacher is having one of the most beneficial of mental health experiences.

Mention was made in the previous discussion of the young child's emotional needs, of his need for assistance from the teacher in building controls. This assistance comes through firm, consistent, yet kindly expectations, and through the setting of definite limits for behavior. The pre-adolescent needs this same support because it takes time for controls to be established. Also, as the child grows older and his experience broadens, he has many new and different situations to meet. He cannot be expected to know how to deal with all of these situations with confidence and self-control by himself. The pre-adolescent has greater self-control, is more able to delay satisfying his impulses, and can tolerate greater frustration than the younger child; he can accept denial of individual wishes when they are opposed to group wishes or well-being. He still, however, needs the help of an adult to get past occasional exciting or disturbing events.

The teacher learns to watch for signals of approaching loss of self-control in the group or the individual, and, by using a firm word of caution, by changing an activity, by interjecting good humor to relieve tension, or by verbally setting limits, he helps the children to maintain the desired control.

Teachers often wonder why children "can't remember" that certain behavior is unacceptable and why they must be cautioned and helped to maintain acceptable behavior. If it were better understood why children "can't remember," teachers would give them support when it is needed without making them feel "bad" or guilty about their "misbehavior."

It takes a long time for children to build controls that are acceptable to group living and adult expectations because they lack the experience to foresee the results of certain behavior and their own desires and wishes seem so important to them. It is good that their own desires and wishes are so strong; this is what enables them to maintain their own integrity as individuals. In this process of building controls, it is essential for good mental health that a balance be achieved: a balance between the individual's own important desires and the kind of behavior that makes for comfortable group living and acceptance by others.

Adults—parents and teachers—need to help children achieve this balance without forcing too much control too early or imposing so much that the child never learns to think for himself or gain self-control. Too much early control brings about repression on the part of the child of his own feelings and wishes. He becomes a creature of the adult's wishes and lives only to please him. Complete freedom to do as he pleases is unrealistic and tends to get the child into difficulty because he rides rough-shod over others, thereby losing their acceptance.

Another of the teacher's functions is to help the child gradually build controls acceptable to our culture, not forgetting that these controls come when the child feels it is important to have the approval of his teacher and his peers. If the teacher, then, recognizes the pre-adolescent's need for continued support and gives it ungrudgingly without being harsh or dictatorial, he will be providing an atmosphere conducive to good mental health.

The thirst for new experience becomes strong during this period, and the teacher who realizes this fact may perform a great service by seeing that the children's interests and curiosities—need for widening horizons—are satisfied. Schools may talk in terms of the curriculum, but by giving the pre-adolescent the opportunity for a wider variety of activities in science, creative arts, literature, and social occasions with peers, they are fostering a good mental health program. The child who can experience satisfaction and joy through many successful activities is acquiring feelings of self-confidence and inner power.

Experiences in and of themselves can be sterile, but those

with people are most significant to mental health. It is the inter-play with other people that builds the self-concept which makes for emotional well-being and mental health. It is a truism that we see ourselves through the eyes of others. As the child sees the teacher and his classmates react to him with affection or rejection, with respect, contempt, or ridicule, so his self-concept and his future mental health are built. At no time in life is the acceptance of peers more necessary to emotional well-being than in pre-adolescence; the teacher who can foster this accomplishes much. The child who cannot accept others or be accepted by them at this stage of life is sure to have serious problems then and later.

The opportunity for creative thinking and creative expression of all kinds is a continuing need for the pre-adolescent. If the significance of creativity were understood, schools would never debate its place in school curricula. It is only through creative acts that the individual is truly himself, and it is only as he is himself that he remains emotionally healthy. No intention is implied here to overlook the necessity for gathering academic skills and getting a background of facts from history, literature, science, and mathematics. One does not become creative in a vacuum or void. Experiences and learning nourish creativity.

The place of competition in the classroom, on the playing field, or in the gymnasium comes in for considerable discussion on the part of both parents and teachers. Where does it stand in relation to the teacher's responsibility for pre-adolescent mental health? It seems a natural desire for all children to want to compete, to win. But it is difficult to determine how much of this is "natural," how much is culturally imposed. Certainly it is true that society is competitive, and children must know how to meet the competition and stand up to it without letting it rule or ruin their lives.

For young children, competition should be minimized; for the pre-adolescent, it should also be de-emphasized, but the child must learn to accept some of it and know how to handle it. It should not be permitted to assume undue proportions in any part of the school life, nor should it be used to stimulate or motivate learning. Children learn better without such motivation, and have better mental health.

Because we live in a competitive society, we cannot shield a child from competition. It would not be wise to do so; this would be unrealistic and render the child unable to handle it when he got out into the world. Schools do not, however, need to emphasize or foster competition. They would do well to help each child develop his unique abilities, learn to accept himself, and come to feel competent and worthwhile. Such a child can meet competition without crumbling, because he feels worthy and accepted. He does not need to "beat the other fellow" in order to bolster his own self-respect. He can rejoice in winning a game or a contest, but he does not *have* to win or feel "no good" if he loses. A self-confident individual can face competition in the world. Schools best prepare children to meet competition by helping them become self-confident through gaining a sense of accomplishment and success.

The pre-adolescent is usually not ready for serious participation in competitive sports. To be forced to take part in competitive sports instead of playing the game for the fun of it places a severe emotional strain upon many of them. Some cannot excel in sports and are at a stage in their emotional development where to fail—and thus gain the displeasure of some of their peers—is devastating. Schools should give serious thought to the custom of requiring pre-adolescents to take part in competitive gym or sport activities if they are truly concerned with developing sound mental health. Surely children can have healthy physical exercise without being forced to take part in competitive physical education.

SUMMARY

In discussing the emotional needs of pre-adolescents, it has been mentioned that they, like younger children, need the teacher's acceptance and support, along with fostering of their natural urge to become more independent and self-controlled.

The importance of peer identification cannot be overstressed, and the teacher's awareness of this process and what he does to foster it are a big part of his function.

Attaining self-confidence through achievement in school tasks is vital at this stage of development, and the teacher's part in helping the child gain this feeling of self-confidence is extremely important. Self-confidence is basic to sound mental health.

Fostering creativity in all its aspects is another of the teacher's main goals. The creative child is living productively, using his abilities, and exhibiting positive mental health.

Excessive competition in the school is harmful, and the need for minimizing it should be stressed.

The pre-adolescent is strengthening his self-concept and needs wise guidance from his teachers in building an image of himself as a person with inner strength and self-confidence—one who is accepted and respected by others.

4

Emotional Needs of the Adolescent

Adolescence covers a wide span of years, and emotional needs vary extensively within this period. The child develops without any sharp line of demarcation from one period of development to the next. A foundation for emotional well-being in adolescence is laid in the years preceding it. While adolescence should be a time for searching and "trying out wings," and while this period may be accompanied by emotional flurries, the child who has passed through early and middle childhood with good adjustment can pass through this stage with minimum upheaval to himself and others. For the purpose of our discussion, let us assume that we have a "well-adjusted" child reaching adolescence. What can the teacher do? What is his part in meeting the emotional needs of this child?

Most of us agree on the ultimate goals of adult (parent and teacher) guidance. We strive to enable the growing child to reach a stage of independent action and control; to gain success according to his interests and abilities; to gain increased confidence in and understanding of himself and others; and to take his rightful place in peer and adult relationships. The teacher's role in this process is a big one.

I suppose we can say that the teacher's first task is to teach or help children gain success according to their interests and abilities. This is an important task. We also must ask how the teacher can accomplish this task most effectively. By being aware of each pupil as an individual and by helping each one grow in emotional maturity, the emotional needs of growing youngsters can be met.

The adolescent needs an opportunity to practice the inner control that he has been building. This is the time when he should have more freedom and should be encouraged and permitted to set up plans for his own conduct and group living. The adolescent should participate as fully as possible in his own "discipline"; thus will he come to see the responsibility of the individual for himself and his relationship to the group. He must be helped to consolidate his gains and be given opportunities to practice concepts of respect for the individual and the group.

These statements do not imply that boys or girls will always be successful in practicing "inner control." Since adolescence —particularly the early stages—is a normal period of disorganization, these children need help from their teachers in planning, evaluating their success, replanning, and occasionally in having firm authoritarian limits set for them. This does not mean that adolescents do not have the ability for self-direction, nor does it imply a lack of respect for them as individuals. Because of their stage of development, however, they may at times lack the judgment, power, or desire to plan and execute what is the best for the group.

Teachers and parents are responsible for advising, suggesting, or even insisting—on occasion—certain courses of action as preferable or necessary. Instances demanding particular behavior or action should become minimal or nonexistent as the pupil reaches upper high school or when self-control becomes consistent.

Youngsters need adult support for control *even* in adolescence. If adult control is minimal and can be counted on, the adolescent feels more safe and secure. He is on the threshold of having to become completely responsible for his actions, and this step is tempting as well as frightening. Teachers should be ready to give support when it is necessary without being annoyed or upset and without overemphasizing the youngster's guilt. When control or correction can be given without hostility, the youngsters derive the greatest benefit from it. Righteous anger is not without its place, but it should be saved for the really important and serious occasions.

Sometimes adolescents refuse to take on a certain responsibility when asked by teachers. If this occurs, the adult should restudy the situation and consider what they are asking. Are they requesting the group to take on something which they feel will hamper their freedom or place them in a position of having to police their classmates? If it is the former, the situation can be resolved only by discussing with the pupils their ideas on freedom and by working through to a solution that all can agree on. If it is the latter case, then the adults need to be critical of their suggestion; no adolescent wants to be placed in a position of policing members of his own group. This stage of development—synonymous with peer identification and rebellion against adult society—precludes such behavior.

Whatever plan is set up with adolescents for conducting their group and individual behavior, it will need mutual understanding and cooperation. Since the approval and respect of their teachers is still important to most adolescents, once there is mutual understanding and respect for each other, the youngsters will use their own inner controls to minimize the need for adult demands. Unless the pupil respects the teacher and feels that the teacher has respect for him, there will be little cooperation. An adolescent who senses a teacher's lack of respect for him as an individual is in an untenable situation in the group, unless he happens to be immensely popular with his peers. In that case, he may sway the group and align it against the teacher.

In helping the adolescent gain success according to his interests and abilities, the teacher must have the help of the school psychologist and the guidance counselor. Unless some measure of a pupil's ability and interest can be gained through intelligence tests and individual interviews, the teacher can-not be certain of the limits of either. Certain aptitude or interest inventories can be used in conjunction with interviews to evaluate interests and abilities at the senior high school level.

The school should be able to help the adolescent gain a feeling of successful achievement even if his ability is limited. This feeling of achievement is a basic principle for good emotional adjustment. To help all children gain it necessitates a flexible and varied program to fit all levels of ability. It also requires collaboration between the home and the school so that clear understanding is obtained and consistent support is given to the pupil. Some children fail even though they have good or superior ability; these pupils will be discussed later.

If the adolescent, during his earlier years, has used his creative ability—and most children have some—his creative thinking and acts should be at a high level. His school program should be one that encourages and fosters this individual creativity so that he can use and continue to develop his own unique powers. Adolescence is a normal period of idealism, of striving for heights, of yearning to know oneself and be oneself. The greatest learning as well as the greatest growth in emotional maturity comes when the individual is using his creative powers in thought and action.

Self-understanding is something that comes slowly. Most adolescents are striving for self-understanding and self-realization. In daily living with classmates and wise, sympathetic teachers, they can gain increased insight into themselves and others. This can be accomplished through association with adults who love youngsters, who have insight into human motivations and feelings, who understand the adolescent's need for hero worship, and who know how to inculcate values without moralizing and lecturing. This is not an easy task, and it takes a truly dedicated person who believes in children and who feels that the emotional and social development of children is an important part of school learning.

Letting youngsters talk about themselves and their feelings is helpful under wise guidance. More important, however, is the living example of fine teachers who can tolerate the hero-worship of some of their pupils who need this identification with them in the process of growing up. The teacher who bears with this identification and does not feed on the attachment for his own emotional needs can be tremendously helpful to the adolescent in his seeking to find out what it means to be grown-up. Growing up often seems mysterious and threatening to some children, and to have the advantage of association with fine teachers who have worked out values, standards, and ways of living that can serve as ideals and patterns is more beneficial than the wisest sermons.

When pupils see teachers treat them with respect and concern for them as individuals, they more easily develop self-respect and respect for others—basic cornerstones of sound mental health and life adjustment.

There is a place for both competition and cooperation in the lives of adolescents. It would be difficult to imagine a world without competition, and the growing child has to learn how to handle it and live with it. This is not competition in the sense that one should strive to out-do the other person with disregard for his feelings and self-respect; rather, it is competition from the standpoint of being realistic about one's abilities and skills.

Adolescents know that in earning a living, certain jobs or professions take certain skills. Either one has the ability to develop a particular skill or one does not. If self-respect, together with respect for all individuals, has been inculcated, the adolescent will do his best in any necessary competitive examinations because he knows they are essential. On the other hand, he will not look down upon a classmate who has less ability than he has. The student of lesser or different ability should be helped to select a job or profession in which he can be happy and successful, and he should not feel less worthy because he could not meet the competitive examinations that some of his classmates passed successfully. Who is to say which skill or which job is more commendable or more beneficial to society?

The cut-throat kind of competition in which one individual is attempting to out-smart all others or to win at all costs has no place in any school program. Normal competition as described above is realistic and necessary. The spirit of cooperation and helpfulness should be fostered in the schools, with competition taking only its normal and rightful place.

SUMMARY

To summarize, we have discussed briefly the emotional needs of adolescents. We have said that teachers can meet these needs of normal youngsters by helping them be successful in their learning and in their relationships with classmates and teachers. They can help them by being truly dedicated individuals who love youngsters and who do not mind being looked to for patterns of behavior, standards, and values. They can help further by guiding the adolescent into stronger and more consistent self-control through the ways discussed. They can help inculcate feelings of self-respect and respect for others. They can help them see the relationship of competition and cooperation in their school life and in the world.

These functions are over and above the teaching of subject matter which goes on all the time. They are the *more than teaching* that was mentioned in the first chapter, and they have always been carried out by teachers concerned with the interpersonal living and emotional well-being of their pupils.

Part Two

Specialized needs of
individual children

5

Symptoms of Unsatisfactory Emotional Development

As the teacher becomes aware of the normal emotional needs of all children, he also perceives the special emotional needs of a few in each group. There are certain children in each classroom whose emotional needs cannot be met in the usual way. Studies show that about 10 per cent of the children in each school fall in this category. For example, in a class of 30, there will be approximately three children who show behavior deviant enough to cause real concern to the teacher. It is true that in some classes you will find fewer disturbed children and in others more, but the average runs as stated above.

This deviant behavior has such symptoms as resistance to learning, extreme dependence on the teacher or classmates, resistance to classroom routine or group living, tantrums, quarreling, fighting, stealing, lying, bragging, bullying, crying, teasing, destructiveness, withdrawal, fear of physical injury, truancy, school phobia, stuttering, and tics.

Children showing these symptoms in the extreme all have problems of interpersonal adjustment. They do not feel right about themselves, and their relationships to others are poor. These are the children who feel rejected, dominated by others, deprived, jealous, or resentful; who have been over-indulged, who have physical defects, who have suffered prolonged illnesses, or who are mentally retarded. All normal children occasionally show some of these symptoms in a mild form. Whether the disturbance is a temporary one which can be overcome with assistance from the teacher and the parents can be determined by the child's past history and his response to the help offered him. The child's age must always be considered in connection with the symptom. What might be serious behavior in an older child may not be so serious in a younger one. The younger child normally lacks the inner control usually found in the older one, and he is not as socially aware of acceptable behavior.

Certain symptoms show extreme interpersonal disturbance and indicate the need for immediate attention, not because the symptom itself is any more disturbing to the classroom than others, but because it connotes severe disturbance within the child that can lead to neurotic behavior patterns or delinquency. Such symptoms are school phobia, truancy, extreme withdrawal from classroom activities—often accompanied by a tendency to remain at home frequently for minor ailments, compulsive stealing, persistent destructiveness, resistance to learning—severe learning disabilities in children of normal and above normal intelligence, excessive restless and hyperactive behavior, severe stuttering and tics, and enuresis.

Teachers are faced with children showing some of these symptoms in varying degrees. The purpose of our next chapters is to discuss the meaning of these symptoms and the ways in which teachers can help these children, either directly through their contacts with the child and his parents or by helping the parents seek outside psychological or psychiatric assistance for the child. If the school is fortunate enough to have psychological services available, the teacher and parent can work with the school psychologist. Increasing numbers of schools are providing psychological services for their children—a commendable step. It is likely that all schools eventually will recognize the necessity for school psychologists as equal to that for school nurses and physicians. Any child showing severe symptoms of the nature described above is seriously disturbed. In order that we not lose sight of the child in discussing his symptoms, we will try to see what the symptom represents from the standpoint of the child's feelings about himself and others.

In any disturbed child we usually find not one symptom but several; the child also may show first one symptom, then another. This is because he is trying to solve his problems—or disturbance—through a groping behavior, and he will try a variety of ways which we see as symptoms. It becomes necessary, then, to discover what the symptom or behavior means to the child, that is, what problem, what personal relationship, what fear or anxiety he is struggling with.

There are certain general concepts having to do with specific symptomology that are helpful to know. These general concepts will be discussed along with detailed discussions of children having specific problems.

Stealing

as a

Symptom

Most teachers of today
see children's stealing in
proper perspective. They
are no longer excessively
horrified, nor do they feel
that the child is neces-
sarily a moral delinquent
doomed to a life of crime.
Stealing is, however, one
of the common symp-
toms noted in certain disturbed children, and it is
being used in this chap-
ter as a means to illus-
trate specific mental
health principles that
will help us understand
other symptoms. Any
other aggressive symp-
tom could be used just as

well, but because stealing is such an "ordinary problem" in the classroom it seems to suit our present need as a vehicle for gaining understanding of special emotional needs of certain children.

If a child is stealing, there are certain things we want to know about him in order to understand the meaning of the symptom:

1. How old is the child?
2. How long has he been stealing?
3. What does he steal?
4. What does he do with the stolen objects?
5. What is the family constellation?
   a) Number of adults in the home, and their relation to each other.
   b) Other children—ages and sex.
   c) Health of parents.
   d) Financial status of family.
   e) Parents working or not working.
6. Does the child have friends, and who are they?
7. Are there other disturbing symptoms present in the child?
8. What are the child's social and recreational activities outside of school?
9. What is his school adjustment—academic and social?

Merely the fact that the child is stealing is not as significant as the total picture that can be gotten from answers to these questions. This total picture is essential to seeing the stealing behavior in true perspective. When we say stealing behavior, we mean the *child* with the stealing behavior; he must be seen as a person living in a certain family and in a certain community.

Largely the product of his environment, the child can be understood only as one understands his environment which includes the people with whom he lives and who love him or hate him, and whom he in turn loves or hates. Let us first try to discuss the significance of these questions, and then go on to descriptions of actual children who stole.

Question 1 indicates the age of the child as important to know. A young child of five, six, or seven may steal or take things and not be showing unduly deviant behavior. It takes young children time to develop concepts of property rights, and, for most of them, taking something that appeals to them merely means they have not learned consistent concepts of property rights. Usually, if the taking of another's property is treated as a learning situation and not as a heinous crime, with the teacher or the parent helping the child return the object to its rightful owner with a firm statement that others do not want him to take their things, the behavior is quickly corrected or "outgrown." If, in spite of several such lessons, the "stealing" continues in children of this age, then other causes must be explored. For example, is the child really deprived, and does he see other children having many things he cannot have? Is the child hungry, if it is food he is taking? If he feels rejected by others, the stealing may be psychological; it represents to him the taking of what others deny him—love, attention, and recognition.

Stealing often begins in a young child when, for the first time, he has to share his mother's attention with a new baby. His stealing means to him a taking of what he sees as being denied to him, or it may be a means of getting even with the parent for denying him all the attention and love which he had in the beginning. Usually the meaning is on an unconscious level, and the child is unaware of why he is stealing. If, however, he learns that the stealing upsets his mother, he may then use it as a conscious weapon to "punish" her for her neglect or desertion, which is how he interprets the new state of affairs.

If the reason for the symptom is discovered through interviews with the parent, then the child can be helped. If he is stealing food because he is hungry, the school may provide a hot lunch at noon and milk and crackers for a snack. If the child feels rejected, the teacher can give him extra attention and affection and try to get the parent to see his needs. This must be done tactfully or the parent will feel resentful. How to have conferences with parents of children presenting special problems will be discussed in another chapter.

If the child feels rejected by the other children and his stealing consists of taking things that belong to them, the teacher should help him win status in the group. Children do not steal from friends or friendly people unless they are deeply disturbed. One boy who had long been rejected by everyone but his grandmother stole from all but her, although he was a chronic, compulsive "thief."

Question 2 asks how long the child has been stealing. This is important to know if it can be answered. If a child has been stealing for several years, it is certainly a more serious symptom than if the stealing is a first offense. The child over eight years of age who shows persistent stealing over a period of time either feels deeply resentful and hostile toward people —family especially—and so tries to hurt them as he feels they have hurt him, or he has been so rejected that he has lost all feeling. This latter child may become the "hardened" or "conscienceless" delinquent who usually needs prolonged care in a treatment center where he can be slowly reeducated and rehabilitated. If his parents, teachers, and community can give him the affection, attention, and supervision available in a treatment center, the child may be helped at home, but this is difficult to do because the people in the community cannot be selected and controlled.

It was stated earlier that emotionally sick children usually show more than one symptom. A child who steals persistently and who feels that people do not accept him has other symptoms. Lying is almost inevitably part of the behavior pattern. Truancy is frequently present in older children. Such a child may show complete withdrawal and indifference in school, or he may be an aggressive bully. When we think of the child's underlying feelings of rejection by others, and his rejection, in turn, of them, we can see why this anti-social pattern of behavior is present.

Questions 3 and 4 will be discussed together. Whenever a child steals, it helps to determine what it is he steals and what he does with the objects. We mentioned the hungry child who steals food and the obvious cure for this. If a child steals money to treat his classmates, he may be trying to win a place for himself in the group. If this seems to be true, the teacher and the mother would be well advised to start a campaign to help the child gain recognition and friendship. While adults cannot make friends for children, they can set the stage to provide opportunities for the child to form friendships. This can be done, of course, only when the child is not too disturbed to profit from such opportunities. There are instances when a child feels temporarily out of things and can be helped to find a niche. This kind of thing happens to children who have moved to a new community in which the incumbent children have strongly-established cliques. Such a child may have positive feelings toward others but is shut out by the cliques. If such a child steals to buy friends, he can be quickly helped by a sympathetic teacher and parent.

A child who steals things he does not need when he either has them or the money to buy them, and then hoards them or destroys them, is showing that he feels rejected or neglected. This is a form of psychological stealing described previously. This child shows a disturbance in his total interpersonal relationships with both children and adults, and he may be sicker than the child who steals to "win friends with treats." It is a "senseless" kind of stealing that calls for expert help, either psychological or psychiatric. Without help, this child's interpersonal relationships will not improve and his poor behavior will persist.

Older girls usually steal to buy pretty clothes, jewelry, or cosmetics. These are the girls who are already delinquent or pre-delinquent. They receive little real affection or understanding from their families, and they often turn to boy friends for proof that they are wanted. In stealing to buy pretty clothes and jewelry they are seeking to attract boys or have already become involved in sex experiences. Such a girl needs treatment to overcome her neurotic pattern. A teacher can be kind and sympathetic, but is often unable to work a real change.

Before leaving the questions of what a child steals and what he does with the stolen goods, we must mention the child who lives in a family or neighborhood where stealing is acceptable behavior. If the child sees his parents and neighbors steal, it will be difficult to get him to change. In some schools, teachers are faced with this very problem. The behavior then must be seen as part of the community mores, and unless some community-wide project is undertaken to better the living conditions and change the familial customs, the teacher is helpless. Some teachers have been successful in helping such children adopt a more acceptable pattern of school behavior by leading them to see that in school the children do not steal from each other. This has been accomplished with little children who lived in such a community.

Answers to the questions dealing with the family constellation help throw some light on why a child is stealing and how much parental support the teacher can gain in working out a plan to help the child. We shall discuss these questions in detail. It is important to know the make-up of a child's family in order to understand him as a person with certain traits and feelings.

Perhaps we should state again at this point that a child shows symptoms of disturbance when his relationships to others are disturbed. For "normal" acceptable behavior in any society, an individual must feel identified with that society; he must feel that the individuals in that society like him, respect him, accept him as one of them, and consider him a worthy member. In turn, he reciprocates these feelings for them. When a child holds these "good" feelings toward himself and others, we say he is identified with them and wants to act in a way that will continue their maintenance and this relationship.

Since the family is the primary society for the child, the pattern for relationships with others is set in the family. We need, therefore, to study the child's family to discover the reasons for his relations with others and his reasons for lack of identification with society.

Anything that occurs within the family to cause a child to feel unloved, neglected, or different from others will tend to make him suffer from emotional conflict and emotional illness. The family in which parents live in harmony, show consideration and love for each child in like measure and for each other, and present examples of consistent social and moral concepts will be the family most likely to have stable, well-adjusted children.

Now to go back to *Question 5* at the beginning of our chapter on stealing behavior and look at some of the items listed. How many adults live in the home? This is important to know because additional adults in the home often cause a lack of harmony between parents. For example, should one of the grandparents live in the home and the parent has not won complete psychological freedom from his or her mother or father, it is hard for the parent to assume rightful control of the children. This is especially true when the grandparent tends to be domineering and is inclined to treat the parent like an irresponsible child. Other relatives can also be a source of conflict, depending upon the nature of their relationship with the parent. When children live with adults who are in conflict, and when they receive contradictory orders and suggestions from several adults, it is confusing to them and difficult to identify firmly with either one of the adults. Firm indentification with a loving parent is essential for the inculcation of "good" behavior and a feeling of being accepted.

Any situation affecting adults in the home will also affect the children for better or worse. If a parent is ill for a prolonged period, this fact can be disturbing to the home and the child. A precarious financial situation that causes such undue concern to the parents that this matter is constantly before the children can be disturbing to the child. If such a child feels out of things because of the poor financial conditions, he may steal unless family solidarity and values are strong. Sometimes, when parents are too concerned over financial worries, the children are pushed aside because the parents' thoughts and energies are too involved with the money worries.

If the home is broken, either through death or divorce, the child is not in a normal situation in relationship to the homes of his companions. This lack of a normal home not only makes the child feel different but also deprives him of the support, care, and example of both parents. Just how this will affect the child emotionally will depend on the way in which the surviving parent can work out the situation to give the child the greatest amount of normal living and affection.

If both parents need to work, and many do today, then the

young child will suffer unless adequate provision is made for his safety and security during their absence. It is well-known what happens to the "latch-key" children who are lonely and wander unsupervised. The only adequate supervision that can be made for young children of working parents is the substitute of a warm, loving, sympathetic "mother" person in the form of a housekeeper or a teacher in a child care center. Unless there can be continuity in the attention of the mother substitute, the child will suffer, for then no one person gives him consistent attention or the feeling that someone cares what happens to him.

We have not discussed the pressures of other brothers and sisters and their effects on a child. The effects, naturally, are quite diverse and depend again on the parents' ability to make each child feel valuable and completely accepted. There is always a certain amount of normal jealousy among all children, each of whom would like to be a parent's "one and only." Handled wisely, however, this jealousy can be minimized and controlled. Ways to help children who are jealous have been discussed by many writers, and an illustration will be given in a later chapter. If a child feels that his brothers and sisters gain more love from the parents than he does, he may steal.

We can say that the only child need not be "spoiled" or "lonely," and that the child with brothers and sisters need not feel excessively jealous. Usually brothers and sisters gain much from each other, and there is great value to be gained from growing up in a family where there are several children. These children can learn to share, to take turns, to be generous and unselfish, and they can have good fun playing together if their ages are not too different.

From this very brief discussion of the family influence on a child's feelings about himself and others it can be seen that it is necessary to have a picture of the child's family in order to understand his reasons for stealing or for showing other symptoms of disturbance. To round out the picture of the child who steals we need the answers to the rest of the questions — 6,7,8, and 9 — which have to do with his total adjustment to school and home environment.

Question 6 asks, "Does the child have friends, and who are they?" We may find the child without friends, and this fact would be well worth noting both in considering the stealing behavior and ways to help him. We may discover that he is part of a gang whose pattern of conduct includes stealing and destructive behavior. The influence of this gang must be taken into consideration in connection with the individual's stealing. We need to bring constructive influences into the life of this child in order to help him. Moralizing and lecturing him would serve no useful purpose because the gang may bring the only accepting companionship the child has. Only as he is helped to find satisfaction in more wholesome activity and gains acceptance by a group whose activities are socially acceptable will he be led away from his non-social behavior and companionships. Sometimes the only way to help such a child is to place him in a treatment center for a period of time. This may be true if the family and community offer no help toward re-education. Of course, it is far better to be able to help a child within his own family and community if this is possible.

Sometimes a child who steals seems to have friends or acquaintances, but on close observation we find that the relationships are tenuous and the child in question gets no real satisfaction from them. He always feels inferior, rejected, or persecuted. If we find this to be true, we must find out why this is so and try to help the child form more satisfying friendships. This is not always easy, especially when the reasons lie within the child — that is, in connection with his feelings toward people in general. Such a child needs to learn that people do like him, and he should be drawn into organized groups in the home community and school. He needs to experience the friendship of an adult who helps him feel accepted, trusted, adequate or confident, and respected as a person. He needs many experiences in group situations with good adult supervision so that he can "learn" how to form satisfying social contacts.

Question 7 asks, "Are there other disturbing symptoms present in the child?" The answer is pretty obvious, and, since we see stealing behavior as a symptom of poor interpersonal relationships, we would expect to find other unsatisfactory social adjustments. By making a complete evaluation of the child's personality patterns we can assess his "assets" and "liabilities" and help him accordingly.

Question 8 asks, "What are the child's social and recreational activities outside of school?" Since the significance of this question has been discussed earlier, we shall enlarge upon it only by saying that children need constructive, healthy, and creative recreational and physical activities provided for them in home, school, and community. In evaluating a child's adjustment, this must be taken into consideration.

Question 9 asks, "What is his school adjustment, academic and social?" Here, too, we can see that the answer to this question determines the help that will be given the child, as well as the prognosis for his recovery. If the answer is positive, it is a healthy sign; if it is negative, it indicates that the youngster's problems are more involved and complex. There is usually no use in tackling learning problems until his personal problems have been solved.

The purpose of the questions we have discussed briefly is to help us see the child as an individual with feelings, drives, and needs, and as a reflection of his total environment. Only as we can do this can we see the meaning of the stealing and go about helping the child who is telling us through his be-havior that "things are not going well for him."

When you have a child who steals, you need to answer the nine questions listed at the beginning of this chapter. Having answered these questions, you will be in a better position to know how much help you and the parent together can give the child and whether you need to call on expert help to give the child sufficient assistance.

THESE CHILDREN STOLE

Peter was a six-year-old living in a foster home because his parents were divorced and his mother was trying to get her-self established financially. He was an only child, and this was his first separation from his mother. Although his foster mother was kind and loving, and although the social worker who had helped the mother find a foster home had also tried to help Peter accept and understand the need for this change in his life, he felt lonely and rejected.

At school he "took" things from the other children or from the teacher's desk. These items were inconsequential, such as a piece of chalk, a crayon, or a bit of food. Peter was clearly showing that he was taking things because he felt rejected; his was a form of psychological stealing. The teacher helped him by giving him extra attention and love and by seeing that he had every opportunity to feel wanted and needed in the group. She asked the foster mother to fix him special snacks for his mid-morning lunch because special delicacies mean love to a small child.

As part of the regular learning situations in the classroom, the whole group had opportunities to learn respect for prop-erty of others — a feeling all six-year-olds need to acquire. This was done through helping each child feel he had "his own" desk, books, and crayons, and that he used "his" while others used "theirs." Children like the feeling of something belonging to them, and it is through this sentiment that they begin to respect the attitude of others toward their special property.

Peter's "stealing" gradually stopped as he felt accepted and wanted by the teacher and the group and as his foster mother was able to give him the security his own mother was unable to provide.

Ann was an eight-year-old who stole things from her classmates and took them home to hoard. She took many things, some new and valuable, such as pencil boxes, an eversharp pencil, a whole new box of crayons, and jewelry. A survey of Ann's total adjustment brought a picture of a deeply disturbed child. She was still wetting the bed at night — enuretic. She was afraid of playing games with others because she felt she could not compete successfully with them, and she had no friends in the neighborhood or at school. She felt she was a bad girl because her parents — especially her father — demanded impossibly mature behavior from her and, as a consequence, she always failed and always felt guilty and unaccepted. She was a finicky eater, and had frightening nightmares.

The teacher could give Ann limited help in the classroom by trying to protect her from the others. She always had Ann return the stolen articles to her after school and then quietly restored them to the rightful owners. The mother always called the teacher to report when Ann brought things home and always had Ann bring them back to school. The teacher also gave Ann some of the accepting attention she so desperately craved by helping her become successful in playing games with the others, by drawing her into group activities wherein she could have a constructive part in using her drawing ability, and by seeing that she gained the feeling of having a real place in the classroom.

Ann had the happiest year she ever had at school, but this was not enough to help her overcome the multitude of symptoms which were still aggravated by the parental attitude mentioned above. It was necessary for Ann and the parent to seek psychological help — therapy for Ann and counseling for the parent.

If such special aid is unobtainable in your community, you will have to be satisfied with limited help and with knowing that school is often the one place where a child may have satisfying experiences. Occasionally, the child and the home are so disturbed that the teacher's help is not effective. The teacher, then, should not think he has failed; rather he should feel that he at least has done all possible, and has been kindly and understanding instead of punitive toward the child.

Roger was fifteen, the third of a family of five children. The family's economic and educational resources were limited. From a small store the father made a marginal income for his family. A man with a violent temper, he tried to rule his children with violence. Roger's relationship with his father was a poor one. His mother tried to stand between the boy and his father's harshness, but, since she was often unsuccessful, the boy blamed her for her inability to save him from beatings and scoldings.

Although his intelligence was average, Roger did not learn well in school. It is hard to learn when one's home life is so unsatisfactory. Consequently, he lost interest in school, and began playing truant. He fell into the company of a similarly unhappy lad, and together they embarked on a plan of outwitting adults. They began stealing and thought it very clever to "put something over" on adults, since the latter seemed to them so unsympathetic and lacking in understanding.

Roger was caught. Since it was his first trip to children's court, he was paroled in the custody of his parents. Although the school tried to help Roger, the long years of parental mistreatment made it hard for him to believe that any adult really cared about him, and he did not respond to his teacher's interest in him. The parole did not work out because the father could not change his attitude toward the boy; consequently, he got into further community difficulty by stealing. When caught this time, he was sent by the court to a training school.

Teachers who, from first grade on, had kept in touch with the parents through conferences or a specially trained person who could have worked with the child and the parents might have prevented the tragedy of his adolescent rebellion against society. We can only speculate. Perhaps you say, "But is this the teacher's or the school's responsibility?" The answer to this question has to be an individual one, but helping such children is part of the teacher's function in meeting emotional needs and is *over and above teaching.*

SUMMARY

As we look at the brief stories of these three children who stole, we see that they were all unhappy, anxious, and lonely. A teacher's part in helping such children would be the same in all instances. He would try to understand the child's reasons for stealing and how he felt about himself and others; he would try to give the child a feeling of acceptance at school, status with his classmates, and greater satisfaction from his accomplishments. With the older child the teacher might try, with the parent's help, to lead him into more constructive behavior through organized group activities both at school and in the community. He would not lecture or moralize, but would help the child realize that although he accepted him, he did not accept his stealing behavior.

As the stories pointed out, sometimes the teacher's understanding and help can be very effective. In other instances, it cannot help. If the teacher cannot be effective in his help, at least he can have the satisfaction of knowing he did not push the child into further unhappiness because of lack of understanding.

7

Aggressive Behavior

The excessively aggressive child can be a source of difficulty for the teacher and the other children in the class. Aggression can be shown in a variety of ways, from harmless but annoying name-calling to the serious bullying and hurting of others. Sometimes, the aggressive child becomes destructive, tearing and smashing others' property. Extreme aggressive behavior in a child of any age is a symptom indicating the child's need for help.

The first emergency

step taken by the teacher — and the principal, if the behavior is really serious — is to set strong limits for the child, telling him that such behavior cannot be tolerated. This measure is for the protection of the other children as well as for him, for, if he persists in his aggressive behavior, he will certainly alienate his classmates and thereby increase his problems.

Unless a child is seriously disturbed, he can usually control excessive aggression if he knows he must. If he cannot control it when strong limits have been set by those in authority, we know he is in urgent need of specialized help. Uncontrollable behavior is a clue to anxieties and anger so great that the child must have help to improve.

People often feel that punishment is the answer for such children. Unfortunately, most of the excessively aggressive children seem to have met with harsh punishment, violence, and lack of understanding on the part of parents and other adults. It is not more *punishment* they need but first, *help* in controlling aggression through strong limits and next, *treatment* and *experiences* with kind but firm adults.

If you have an excessively aggressive child in your class, it would be well to ask a number of questions about him, just as you did about the child who stole. For example, answers to the following questions are helpful in understanding the child and getting at the reasons for his behavior. We must know the reasons if we are going to help him.

1. How old is the child?
2. How long has he shown this pattern of behavior?
3. How does he show his aggression?
4. What is the family picture? (See the discussion on family in the chapter on stealing.)

   a) Does the child receive the affection, attention, and guidance he needs for his age and stage of development?

  b) Are there brothers and sisters in the family, and, if so, what is this child's relationship to them?

  c) Is he as well accepted by the parents as the other children are, or do the parents show favoritism toward one of the other children in the family?

5. Does the child have any friends, and if so what is his status and relationship with them?

6. How does he spend his time outside of school?

7. Does he show other disturbing symptoms besides his aggressiveness? For example: Is he truant from school; does he steal; does he fail in his school subjects; does he have any physical defects that would cause him difficulty in establishing good peer relationships?

A study of these questions makes it clear that we are trying to discover what in the life of the child has disturbed his interpersonal relations with others. The youngster who has good feelings about his own worth and acceptance by others does not have to fight people as the aggressive child does. His aggressive behavior means that he feels people have pushed him aside, have been unfair to him, have not given him the love and understanding that all children need. He is, therefore, both fearful and angry. He is afraid of not being acceptable and he is angry at being denied this acceptance. When we are angry, we want to hurt others as we feel they have hurt us. As children strike out in blind anger — aggressive behavior — they fail to see that their behavior gets in the way of acceptance. That is one reason for stressing the first step of setting firm limits for this child.

Setting limits must be only the first step, however. If we really wish to help the child, we must seek answers to the questions listed above. To get these answers, we must have several conferences with the child's parents. The teacher — or the guidance counselor or psychologist, if their services are available to the school — can get these answers.

As the teacher sets limits and strives to get answers to these questions, he should try to establish a good relationship with the child. Naturally, the way the teacher goes about this will depend upon the age of the child, but he will endeavor to show the latter that he likes him, is fair to him, and is trying to help him gain status with his peers. As the teacher does this, he will kindly but firmly refuse to tolerate the disturbing behavior. Children respond more quickly to limits when the teacher shows he is fair, consistent, and accepting. By *accepting* I mean accepting the child as an individual who "belongs" to the group and who is wanted there. Teachers should not be afraid to show children that they like them, and this can be done without being sentimental or making the child conspicuous. Children of all ages respond to a smile, a tone of voice, good humor, patience, and fairness. Little children sometimes need the closeness of physical contacts — a pat, the straightening or tying of a bow, or an arm around the shoulder. Five- and six-year-olds sometimes need to sit on the teacher's lap for comfort and security.

If the teacher can establish a good relationship with the child he will be accomplishing two things: he will show the child that he likes him, something he desperately needs to know, and he will help him gain self-control. It is easier to accept limits from people who like you, and, if the relationship is strong enough, the child will begin to want to please the teacher — the beginning of self-control. If the child feels the teacher really likes him, this in itself can be a truly therapeutic experience. The teacher also needs the aid of parents in his work with the child, and through conferences they can find reasons for the behavior and make plans to help the child.

DISCUSSION OF QUESTIONS LISTED FOR CONSIDERATION

The child's age has an important bearing on the significance of aggressive behavior. We expect more such behavior from younger children who are still building controls. Even here, though, there is a difference between the youngster who occasionally fights or becomes destructive and the one whose typical behavior pattern is one of extreme aggression. We need to consider how habitual the aggressive behavior is and how it affects the child's relationships to others.

The young adolescent may become unexpectedly aggressive for a time as he reaches the stage of development at which he rebels against authority and excessive discipline or control. It helps to know, then, whether the aggressive behavior is a sudden and new development or a pattern of long standing. Unless behavior becomes startlingly deviant, the adolescent usually "finds his head" and levels off. Sometimes he needs more opportunity to be self-directive and independent, and, if given this opportunity, may settle back into his usual, normal pattern.

If the young adolescent becomes startlingly aggressive and the behavior seems out of character for him, it is well to seek a specialist's advice. The behavior might signify a serious emotional disturbance needing specialized treatment. When a younger child becomes suddenly and unexpectedly aggressive, we should look for some unusual pressure or occurrence, either at home or at school, that is causing him to feel pushed aside or unacceptable. The teacher and the mother need to explore the home and school situations together to see if they can discover the source of disturbance.

If aggressive behavior has been present for several years along with other disturbing symptoms, we know that the child's

home and school environment have been poor for some time
and that he will need considerable help. The school environment is purposely included in this statement because, even
though the focal source usually lies in the home relationships,
such a child ordinarily has poor school relationships, too. This
is inevitable because he brings his interpersonal problems to
school with him. Unless he has had an unusually understanding teacher and principal, the school has aggravated rather
than helped his behavior. This is less true today as school personnel begin to understand the causes for disturbing behavior
and take different attitudes toward the children showing this
behavior.

The child with a long history of aggressive behavior usually
cannot be helped successfully by the teacher; rather, he needs
treatment. It is well for the teacher to know this in order to
be better prepared to cope with the situation. After doing all
of the things described above, he should not feel to blame if
he is unable to go beyond the first step of setting limits. Instead of using punitive and hostile methods to gain control,
he should let the situation set the limits. For example, he can
firmly state, "This cannot be done in our school," rather than
lecturing, moralizing, or becoming retaliatory toward the child.

The number of ways in which the child shows aggression
and the violence of his behavior will help us understand how
fearful and angry he is. The aggressive child is always afraid
down underneath; he fears that he is unworthy, bad, and unacceptable to others. The extent and the quality of his aggressiveness, therefore, will let us know how disturbed the
child is and how hard we will have to work to help him.

From conferences with parents, we hope to find out what it
is that is causing the child's problems. It is not always easy to
determine if a child has poor relationships with his parents
and brothers and sisters. The parents may not be harsh or

violent with him, but they may show in many subtle ways that they dislike him or are dissatisfied with him. Constant criticism, nagging, and unfavorable comparison with other children are all ways in which parents show the lack of secure, constant affection and acceptance. Often, parents feel that they act this way toward a child to help him improve in conduct, manner, or achievement, while unconsciously they are showing lack of genuine affection and tearing down the child rather than building him up.

Since all children must have genuine affection and acceptance from their parents, they will strive to get it if it is denied them. The aggressive child is striving to get attention as a substitute for the affection, or he is consciously or unconsciously punishing others because parental neglect or rejection makes him feel that all people reject him. Eventually they do, if his behavior continues disturbing. Ordinarily the "punishment" of others is on an unconscious level. The child is unaware of what it is that makes him strike out at others. He usually says, "They do not like me," or "They are not fair."

If the child has been disturbed for a long time and thinks it hopeless to gain good relationships with others, he may say, "I don't care. I don't like them." Occasionally a child is conscious of what he is doing in his aggressive behavior and will verbalize it when he is talking to someone he has learned to trust. If his motive is on a conscious level, it can be met in a straightforward way when parents and teachers demonstrate to him that they like him and help him have satisfying experiences with others. This process takes time and must be accomplished gradually over a period of many months.

It is important to know whether the child has any friends at all and, if so, the status of the friendships. A child who is able to form some friendships — unless these are undesirable gang members who are also fighting society — is less disturbed emotionally than the one who has no friends. If he is able to form a satisfying relationship with someone, then he is more easily helped because he can form an attachment to or identification with other people.

If it is discovered that the youngster has no close peer associations other than membership in a destructive, aggressive gang, then strong measures are needed to help him. Identification with an anti-social gang is not easy to change, for the youngster has gained some self-respect and acceptance as a member of a gang. He will be loathe to give up this association unless something else as satisfying can be offered as a substitute. Youth leaders trained in working with delinquents or pre-delinquents are often successful in helping such children. Sometimes these aggressive youths are helped only through removal from the community and placement in a treatment center; these are the extreme cases. There are many children who can be helped by their parents and teachers.

AGGRESSIVE CHILDREN

Tommy was one of a pair of fraternal twins. From the beginning, the other twin was the "good" one and found acceptance from his parents. Tommy, by temperament more active and strong-willed, caused his parents trouble, and, when they saw how placid and amenable the brother was, they began holding him up as a model for Tommy. They also punished Tommy severely for his "naughtiness," and found that he became even naughtier. He would have temper tantrums; he would be disobedient, noisy, and untruthful.

In first grade Tommy was a source of annoyance to the classroom. He was loud; he interrupted constantly; he found it hard to sit still. On the playground he teased and bullied the other children until they became afraid of him.

Conferences with the mother elicited her feelings that Tommy was a bad boy and that she and her husband did not know what to do with him. They punished him severely for his badness, but it did no good. The twin brother was a model of behavior, and they could not understand why Tommy could not be like him. The mother said she was almost a nervous wreck over Tommy and that her husband was desperate.

Following this conference, the teacher tried in every way to help Tommy feel that he was a "good" boy, that he was wanted in the classroom, and that the children would like him too. She set firm limits against the fighting and bullying on the playground, saying he could not fight like that at school, and she redirected his energy into constructive play.

The mother, with her husband's help, began to change the family's attitude toward Tommy. They stopped calling him bad, stopped the unfavorable comparison with the twin brother. They began planning constructive and happy experiences with Tommy. Gradually, they changed their relationship to him from a critical, punitive one to a happier, more positive one.

With the joint efforts of the school and the home, Tommy became less aggressive as he found people accepting him. By the end of the first grade, considerable progress had been made and Tommy had become relaxed enough to make a beginning in learning to read. A continuance of the same attitude by the second grade teacher, working jointly with the parents, brought steady improvement in Tommy's behavior and learning. It was mentioned earlier in this book that good adjustment and learning usually go hand-in-hand; this was clearly demonstrated in Tommy's case.

John showed his anger and fear in another way. He was nine and in the fourth grade. He was a disruptive force in the classroom. Shouting out at any time, he would interrupt the teacher and the other children whenever he felt like it. He would sing, whistle, and bang things. He would get into a loud argument with a classmate whenever he was displeased, and this was often. Since he found it hard to sit still — he was so tense and hyperactive it was really impossible at times — the teacher gave him permission to go for a drink of water or take a walk down the hall when he became too restless. Abusing this privilege, he left and re-entered noisily, either banging the door or shouting out something to someone across the room. He lost his temper frequently. Always, he felt others were "unfair" to him.

The teacher tried setting limits for John and giving him extra attention for acceptable behavior. She achieved temporary and unpredictable improvement which lasted a day or only half a day. Next, she held a conference with the parents to see if she could determine the reasons for John's behavior. In this conference it was discovered that John was the youngest of three children, there being a brother aged fifteen and a sister aged seventeen. The father had his own business, and during the past two years the mother had been helping the father. This meant that John was left under the supervision of his older sister and brother in the afternoons; many times he was unsupervised because they were busy with their own affairs. It also meant that his mother was tired and impatient with him at night and called him bad. On top of all this, John's older brother won acclaim for his baseball in high school and was given much praise and attention by the family. John felt pushed aside, neglected, and bad because of his relationship with his parents.

The parents were eager to help John. The present situation had come about gradually and without their being aware of what was happening. It was only when they began giving John his share of their attention and acceptance and stopped calling him a bad boy that the teacher saw an improvement in John's behavior at school. If the teacher had been unable to gain the parents' concern and desire to build a better relationship with John, her attempts at school would have been unsuccessful.

The above two case histories illustrate how teachers can help meet the emotional needs of children. Conferences with parents and conscious efforts to help the children rather than punish them were actions on the teacher's part *over and above teaching.*

Teachers cannot always be so successful in their efforts. Take the story of *Andy,* a third grader, who showed exactly the same behavior as John. His teacher took the same steps as John's teacher, but was unable to get the helpful understanding of Andy's parents. They were too immature, too neurotic themselves to be able to change their attitude toward their two boys, one of whom was younger than Andy. The mother was home all day, but she had little understanding of children. Her method of discipline was first to tolerate certain behavior laughing at it and thinking it funny; then, when her patience gave out, she would scream at the children and strike out.

The mother consented to psychological help for Andy, and the school psychologist worked with him in weekly sessions for a year. The mother was seen for counselling on an irregular basis when she saw the need for help with home problems. Andy showed steady improvement, and in fourth grade was a calm and contributing class member. He would not have shown this great improvement without treatment.

This brief story about Andy is told not to discourage teachers but to help them feel less frustrated and less guilty when they find they cannot solve all problems with their pupils. If a school psychologist had not been available or if Andy's mother had been unwilling for him to have treatment either through the school or on a private basis, the teacher would have been very limited in what she could accomplish. Sometimes teachers have to face this fact and accept it. But perhaps they can learn to live with their children on a non-punitive, non-hostile basis when they understand the meaning of the symptoms. Tommy, John, and Andy were all fearful, angry boys. Such children see hostility on the part of adults as further evidence that they are disliked and bad.

Ernie, a ninth grader, behaved so aggressively that he had to be excluded temporarily from the classroom. An immediate conference was held with the parent by the principal. It was explained to the parent that punishment would not help Ernie, but that he was excluded because he had to realize that his aggressive behavior could not be tolerated. He was endangering both himself and others. Ernie was told that he could return to school when he was sure he would control his behavior. He returned to school after two days, and the principal and teacher made a great effort to make him feel welcome and needed. Ernie was given considerable attention for constructive actions, and he gained much satisfaction from the approval of the adults and his peers.

In a conference with the father, the principal suggested that he take some interest in Ernie. The father was unable to respond to this suggestion, father and son having had a poor relationship for a number of years. At least one thing was accomplished, however; the father stopped nagging Ernie and permitted him to have more freedom of action. The school, through hobby clubs and sports, drew Ernie into more satisfactory group living. His behavior at school became quite acceptable and his school marks improved.

This story was given as an illustration of what can be accomplished with older children as well as with younger ones if the school takes its responsibility for emotional health seriously. All Ernies do not turn out so well, but it is always worth a try.

EXCEPTIONS

Occasionally a child's behavior is very aggressive because he is "spoiled" or pampered and has never had limits set for him. Usually these children have had good experiences with people and can have their behavior redirected by the teacher who has patience and good humor. Such a child, always the center of attention for adoring parents and grandparents, has to learn acceptable group behavior. This can be accomplished more easily if the teacher "retrains" him in a non-hostile way, kindly but firmly letting him know that he likes him but that there are certain rules of behavior in a group to which all must adhere.

Another exception is the child who comes from a home or a neighborhood where everyone pushes, shoves, grabs, and quarrels as a regular pattern of behavior. This child is acting as he has been taught to act through imitation. He, too, needs retraining by a patient, kindly teacher who helps him see that in school everyone is considered and no one has to "fight" for his rights. He needs many experiences in which he can see that each person in the class has rights and responsibilities. If this lesson can be learned with the help of a loving teacher, it will be accepted more quickly.

SUMMARY

We can say that excessively aggressive behavior usually indicates a fearful, angry child who is fighting to get what he feels has been denied him. Only by recognizing the meaning of the behavior and taking steps to help the child overcome his fear and his anger can his behavior be improved. Teachers, with the parents' cooperation, can often help these children improve their relationships to others, improve their feelings of self-worth and confidence, and make them better adjusted, contributing group members. It takes time to accomplish this with many children, and it needs the concerted help of all the school personnel — the present teacher, the principal, and next year's teacher, too. Thus can the children receive consistent understanding and guidance. If the school has the services of a psychologist and a guidance counselor, these specialists can be called upon for help with the most serious problems.

Withdrawing Behavior

For some reason or other, parents and teachers alike have become very concerned about what they call the "withdrawn child." To them the term connotes serious emotional disturbance, but they are not sure just what it signifies. Perhaps the best way to reach a decision on this matter is by getting a complete picture of the child in his total environment. By doing this, one is able to answer certain important questions. For example:

1. Does the child always play alone, or stay

by himself both at home and at school? Does he go home from school day after day and stay by himself, reading or playing with toys in a solitary manner?

2. Does he have any friends — even one or two?
3. What are his interests?
4. What community activities does he participate in?
5. Does the child have many fears? (Since all children have some fears, one would need to know their degree and extent.)
6. Does the child take part in school activities? Does he volunteer to recite in class or serve on a committee? Does he play games with the children, and, if so, does he initiate the game or does he follow others' suggestions?
7. Does the child seem to be lost in daydreams much of the time?
8. Does he live in a make-believe world much of the time?
9. Is he learning what is expected of a child his age?
10. Does he seem happy most of the time?

An inventory of these questions will help determine if the child is truly isolated and if he is living too much within himself, preoccupied with his fantasies.

If a child — of any age — has no friends, never plays with others in school or at home, never volunteers to recite in class or to serve on committees, daydreams excessively, or has too many fears, he is indeed withdrawn and needs help. Some children are quiet and more gentle than others, and this may be in keeping with their normal temperament. But all children — even quiet, gentle ones — should have friends and play with others. It is the child who has no friends and who is preoccupied with fantasies that should cause us concern. Children do not need to have hordes of friends or be the life of the party to be "normal" and well-adjusted. Some of them are happy with one or two friends and with quieter, less boisterous activities. If the teacher and the parent think through the questions listed above, they usually have no difficulty in determining whether or not a child is abnormally withdrawn.

It is well to get a picture of the total environmental behavior because we sometimes find different behavior patterns in school as opposed to the home. A child may be rather quiet and shy at school but active and the center of a play group in his neighborhood. This is not the usual pattern, but it occurs often enough to warrant a word of caution. In studying children, we should get a picture of their behavior in many situations and not come to hurried conclusions based on too few or too brief observations.

When we find some children who seem unusually quiet and withdrawn, our first question is, "How serious is this behavior?" And following close upon this comes the query, "How can we help him?" It may not be easy to decide just how serious the behavior is without expert advice, but the teacher and the parent can get a pretty good idea if they explore with the above questions carefully.

Causes of serious withdrawing behavior usually lie within the interpersonal relations between parents and child. Something causes the child to be fearful of not being acceptable to his parents and to others, so he gives up trying to please or get attention and withdraws into a fantasy world where he can arrange things more pleasantly. Sometimes a physical handicap prevents a youngster from playing games or being normally active. He may withdraw unless he is helped to gain a feeling of belonging in the group for other skills or contributions.

A "slow-learner" who has suffered failure and lack of acceptance by classmates and teachers may become withdrawn in school. The withdrawing behavior is then an indication of the child's feeling of being a failure in the eyes of his teacher and classmates.

Teachers must be careful not to overlook possible school experiences that push children into a pattern of withdrawal for avoiding painful situations. Such a child tends to live in a world of fantasy that is more pleasant than reality. He withdraws from contacts with others which he feels will show him at a disadvantage.

For most withdrawn children, causative factors lie in the feeling of being worthless and unacceptable to parents and then flow over into relationships with others. The seriously withdrawn child is depressed, anxious, and fearful. He also carries a load of anger and resentment toward others which is usually deeply repressed. The anger comes from being unacceptable to others — as he believes he is — and, since he considers it dangerous to feel angry toward others, the feeling is repressed into the unconscious. Parents and teachers sometimes see this child as very good, quiet, and amenable. They do not realize that it is his discouragement and fear that make him so "good." Such children may occasionally have outbursts of anger, with tears or tantrums. This behavior puzzles the teacher or parent, for they can see no apparent reason for the outburst. The reason is not immediately obvious because the precipitating incident is usually a minor one. The real cause is the load of anger and fear that lies underneath and accumulates until some explosion is inevitable. If the child is asked the reason, he will give some trivial surface explanation that makes little sense or has little bearing on the actual cause.

Parents and teachers consider a withdrawn child more seriously disturbed emotionally than an aggressive child. This is because they tend to associate withdrawing behavior with a mental illness, *schizophrenia*. While it is true that a schizophrenic child may go through a stage of being quiet and solitary, this is not always the case. The schizophrenic child may be hyperactive, aggressive, and destructive in behavior at certain times. It behooves parents and teachers, therefore, not to attempt to reach an independent conclusion, but to seek counsel if a child's behavior is excessively deviant. Although the quiet, solitary child may be seriously disturbed, he may need just warmth and encouragement to expand and "pull out of his shell." Many teachers have seen quiet, shy children do precisely this as the result of affection and kindly interest. If this happens and the child begins to learn and participate in regular classroom activities, cause for concern may cease. It is well to watch these children for the next few years, however, and to remain alert for signs of possible regression. It is only through steady progress in learning and social adjustment that we can be sure the child's emotional health is satisfactory.

In speaking of serious withdrawing behavior, it was stated that the cause must be sought within the interpersonal relations between parents and child. Parental rejection is one of the main sources of contagion, and it is difficult to alter. Often, the rejection is on an unconscious level and the parent is totally unaware of it. Teachers are usually not very successful in helping mothers see this rejection or in helping them change, for it is the mother's own neurotic and immature personality that is causing her to reject her child. She cannot change unless she gets help for her own personal problems.

A moderately withdrawn child — this evaluation often is a subjective one — can frequently be helped by the teacher, and his mother often makes beneficial changes in her attitude toward the child once she is aware of the need to do so. It may be useful to give some illustrations at this point to help distinguish between the moderately withdrawn child and the seriously withdrawn one. The younger the child, the more easily he can be helped to "come out of his shell." A seriously withdrawn child in junior or senior high school has had many years of unsatisfactory personal relationships and usually needs intensive treatment to improve.

Joan was in the fourth grade of a village school. The teacher noted that she was an unusually quiet child: she did not speak to the other children; she did not play with them. The children ignored her because she so successfully pulled within herself. In an endeavor to help Joan, the teacher tried giving her special tasks or "privileges" such as watering the plants, going on errands, passing the paper, etc. Joan did these things mutely and with no show of interest.

When the teacher decided this treatment was not helpful, she invited the mother for a conference. The mother told the teacher that Joan was the oldest of four children and as such she was given much responsibility at home. The mother leaned on Joan to help watch the younger ones, to dust, to wash the dishes, and to run errands to the store. No wonder Joan did not see the teacher's "privileges" as such; this was more of the same work she had at home! The teacher talked to the mother about her concern over Joan's withdrawing, silent behavior, and together they wondered if perhaps Joan was too burdened for a nine-year-old. She probably felt the others were getting much more than she was from the parent. They were free and were taken care of while Joan was always asked to be helpful and had to take care of herself.

Teacher and mother tried to plan ways to help Joan be more carefree and childlike. The mother planned to give Joan less responsibility and more "fun." The teacher watched for opportunities in the classroom. The chance came when a gentle girl introduced puppets into the classroom. The teacher brought Joan and this other child together to work on puppets. From this contact the two girls developed a friendship. They made puppets and put on a play for the class. Joan would do this because she could hide behind the theater. The two girls exchanged visits after school and one or two others joined them. By the end of the year, Joan was still "shy" but no longer the silent, solitary child she had been in the fall.

Since the school was a small one, the fifth grade teacher was informed about Joan by the fourth grade teacher, and the same help was extended to Joan again in fifth grade. Joan made a good adjustment and continued to be a friendly and contributing member of the class. Her special friend of fourth grade and several others went with her to fifth and sixth grades; she was not separated from them as she was promoted from grade to grade. This was wise planning on the part of the school. A child who has difficulty in forming friendships should not be separated from his friends as he moves to the next grade.

Edward, in the fifth grade, was called to the attention of the school psychologist. He was a seriously withdrawn child who participated in none of the classroom tasks. He did none of the work assigned to the class, and he never worked or played with others. He refused to go to his gym classes. He came to school only because his parents insisted.

Although Edward was so withdrawn, he frequently became disturbing to the class because of his emotional explosions, during which he would shout out defiantly and angrily if the teacher tried to draw him into some activity. He would not work himself; neither did he want to let others work. The teacher tried in every possible way without success to interest Edward and help him feel a part of the group.

Upon investigation the psychologist found that Edward's school work had begun to show a slump the previous year in another school. She also found that he suffered frightening nightmares which kept him from going to sleep night after night. He felt completely worthless and unacceptable to his parents and to others. Inwardly, he harbored the most intense feelings of anger and hatred toward his parents and toward teachers — who represented authority figures to him, as did his parents. He also felt angry toward his classmates because he thought they were rejecting him and saw him as no good — the way he saw himself.

Although Edward had intelligence in the upper range of the

superior level, he achieved absolutely nothing in school. The teacher found it impossible to help him or to draw him out of his world of fantasies about himself and others.

The school psychologist was able to convince the parents that psychiatric treatment was necessary for Edward. After two years of treatment he showed considerable improvement, but was still a quiet, seclusive person. His school work varied from excellent to poor, but he always passed at the end of the year.

Edward was a seriously withdrawn boy, one whom no teacher could help. He was an emotionally ill youngster who needed prolonged treatment over a period of years. The prognosis for such seriously disturbed children is uncertain, but psychiatry is able to help many of them lead fairly normal, productive lives.

When a teacher has such a disturbed child in his class, he must use all resources available to help him. If there is no psychologist in the school, the teacher and principal together usually determine the best steps to take. Sometimes psychiatric consultation and treatment are available through community resources, and parents can be directed there for assistance.

The two illustrations above show the degrees of withdrawing behavior and the results when teachers tried to help. In Joan's case, teachers and parents were successful; in Edward's case they could not be. When a child responds fairly soon, as Joan did, the teacher can feel confident of his ability to help. When he does not respond — as Edward did not — the teacher should realize that he has a seriously disturbed child and should call upon the school psychologist or attempt to get the parent to seek private consultation and help.

The many reasons for Edward's serious disturbance were centered in the conflicts in parental and parent-child relationships. They were of long standing and so deep-seated — on an unconscious level — that the parents were unable to understand them or to do anything about them until they, too, took part in the treatment process.

Teachers so often blame themselves for a child's difficulties that it is important for them to know that most very serious behavior problems are the result of family relationships and conflicts. Teachers feel the effects of these conflicts in the classroom, but they are *not* responsible for them.

Teachers should not blame parents for a child's problems, however, but should realize that they generally are confused and unaware of the reasons for their child's deep emotional problems. When talking to parents, the teacher's role should be one of helping them see the full extent of the child's disturbance, and obtain proper consultation.

It is usually better for the teacher not to state that treatment for the child is essential, but to leave that decision to the consulting psychologist or psychiatrist. Teachers cannot always know whether treatment is advisable or not, and should not place themselves in the position of making a statement subject to contradiction later by a specialist.

By understanding causes for deviant behavior, teachers can free themselves from self-blame. They can become more accepting and less hostile toward the suffering child. This, of course, does not mean that they will condone bad behavior; they merely will deal with it firmly, untinged with feelings of failure or guilt. When a teacher is able to deal with disruptive behavior without this personal involvement, he will be more successful in coping with it.

SUMMARY

In trying to aid withdrawn children, it is usually best to put help on an inconspicuous and impersonal basis. Because of his poor self-concept and his feeling of being unworthy of notice, the truly withdrawn child cannot stand having conspicuous attention directed toward him. It may make him pull even deeper within himself. Using other shy and gentle children in the classroom to help the withdrawn one is often effective, as in the case of Joan. Often another child can elicit a response from the withdrawn youngster when an aggressive child or the teacher is unable to.

Teachers have an important role to play in meeting the emotional needs of withdrawn children. By understanding the causes of this behavior, they are better able to help these "silent ones" in the classroom. Frequently, when parents and teachers plan together, they are successful in leading withdrawn children into happier relationships with others.

9

School Phobia; Fear of Coming to School

School phobia would be called more properly *fear of leaving mother.* From k i n d e r g a r t e n through high school we find children who have a hard time coming to school. We must distinguish, however, between those who dislike school because the program is not suited to them, thus causing them to experience repeated failure and loss of status with themselves and others, and those who suffer acute panic in relation to school itself. These latter children are usually bright, capable children who can — and often do — achieve well in school.

Children who suffer from school phobia and find it difficult and sometimes impossible to come to school are usually afraid to leave home to go any place, although some of them can go to gatherings where they are allowed to remain inconspicuous and not asked to achieve or perform in any way. These children cannot leave their mothers and do not want their mothers to leave them. Their real fear is not fear of school but of letting the mother out of sight. Since the reasons for this fear are hidden or repressed, the overt symptom — fear of school — is the behavior that causes teachers concern.

School phobia arises from disturbed parent-child relationships and is, like all serious disturbances, very complex to unravel. Since, in these instances, we find the mother and child bound up in a painful emotional relationship, it is often difficult for the teacher to give much help. These are the children and parents who usually need specialized guidance and therapy.

The basis of most of these unhappy parent-child relationships appears to be the mother's own unhappy marriage; of course, there are many reasons for this latter condition. The end result, however, is that mother and child become tied together in a "dependency-resentment" relationship from which neither can break free.

The child's fear of leaving the mother — and hence of coming to school — indicates that his resentment and revenge fantasies toward the rejecting, non-supportive mother are so strong that he believes they will come true. He must stay near the mother to see that his bad wishes toward her do not come true. Additional complicating factors are involved in each individual instance. A further complication is that because of these "bad wishes" the child believes he is a very bad and worthless person. He thinks others must think he is bad, too, and that they will not like him or accept him. This thought contributes to his fear of coming to school.

School phobia, then, is not basically a fear of school at all, but a symptom revealing the child's feelings of being rejected by the mother and in turn by others because he believes he is bad. What can the teacher do to help such a child?

Before the teacher can do anything to help, the child must, of course, be in school. It is far better for him to be in school than at home, and if the school and the father together state firmly to the child that he must come to school, this firmness will often be enough to keep him coming. The mother is almost always unable to take a firm stand because her own emotions are so involved with the child's. Once he is in school, the teacher can try to help him in a number of ways, depending upon his age.

A small child with school phobia can sometimes be helped by being made the teacher's pet. He is hungry for love from a kindly, supporting adult, and, although the teacher cannot make up for the mother's inability to give the child what he needs, he can help in great measure. Some teachers object to this suggestion, saying that the other children will notice and protest. Perhaps the teacher's special attention will not be so noticeable if he is the kind of person who is able to give all of his children a feeling of being wanted and important in the classroom. Of course this suggestion will work only if the teacher can accept it as valid and can carry it out without feeling unfair to the rest of the class. I have known many teachers able to follow this suggestion with good results to the fearful child and without harming the rest of the class.

The teacher can help the little child feel that he needs him there, and can plan interesting things for him to do to keep him busy. He can help this child, who feels he is bad because of his "bad feelings" toward his mother, learn that others think of him as being a good child. He can tell him what a good boy he is and how much they all like him.

Sometimes these children find it hard to compete with others; they are so fearful that people will not like them, they dare not compete and possibly win. If they won, they would be afraid that the other children would reject them further. It is best for the teacher to see that they have fun in activities without having to "play to win."

If the teacher and the mother are working together to help the child come to school, the mother can assure the child that she wants him to go to school, that she knows *he* will be all right when he is away from her, and that *she* will be all right while he is away from her. This is very important, for he is afraid that his bad wishes toward her might come true in his absence. The mother will need to do this repeatedly over a long period of time. If she can do this and if the father can take a strong positive stand toward the child's going to school, he will gradually gain the feeling that it is good for him to be there.

Teachers can help older children by telling them they want them to be in school and that they miss them when they are absent. The older child will be suspicious, and the teacher must follow this statement by concrete evidence, such as appointing the child to a committee on which he will be contributing to the classroom in what he can feel is an important and necessary way. It is always harder to reach older children in this manner. The suggestion may or may not work, depending upon a number of factors, such as the child's ability to respond to such an approach and the teacher's ability to respond to the child in a genuinely and sincerely interested manner. It is not always possible for the teacher to do this because he may not be able to like the child no matter how much he tries. This is no condemnation of the teacher; it is merely a statement of fact. Also, the child may be too anxious and fearful to be able to respond to the teacher's help.

Everything the teacher can do to make the child feel accepted at school and successful in his work will benefit the child with school phobia. It has been our experience, though, that the child never really recovers from the phobia without treatment. The treatment seems essential to help the child work through the difficult relationship with the parent and his concomitant feelings of being bad and worthless. Therefore, if the teacher or the guidance specialist — either counselor or psychologist — can be instrumental in helping the family obtain treatment for the child, this will be the very best step to take.

In some schools where there is an adequate psychological staff, the psychologist provides treatment for the child when there are no community facilities available or if the family is unable to provide private treatment. This step implies that the school psychologist has had the necessary training to do therapy.

KINDERGARTEN CHILDREN AND FEAR OF COMING TO SCHOOL

Sometimes we find kindergarten children who are afraid to come to school. Not always a school phobia, this certainly indicates that the child does not want to leave his mother. It may be that a new baby has been born recently, and that the child does not want to leave the mother and baby home together while he is at school. He is far too jealous and too afraid of losing more of the mother's love and attention to the newcomer.

A teacher who has time to explore reasons for the little child's reluctance to come to school can often discover such a reason, and she and the mother can do much to help the child feel better about coming to school. The teacher can make the youngster feel very welcome; she can have the class talk about baby brothers and sisters so the little boy or girl will get the feeling of others, too, having to share their mothers. The mother can help most by being sure to give the kindergarten child special, individual attention when the new baby is out of the way — asleep or being cared for by the father — so there will be no interruptions. This will help assure the child that his mother does not love him any less for having a new baby in the house.

Both the teacher and the mother can verbally recognize the child's feelings of jealousy and let him understand they know he feels afraid that his mother won't have time to love him so much. They will emphasize that this is not true, and, of course, the mother must then prove this by giving the child the daily individual attention mentioned in the previous paragraph.

The child should be helped to come to school by the parents — especially by the father — who must make it clear in a matter-of-fact way that going to school is the expected thing for a child his age. By doing this and by giving the child constant reassurance of their love in deeds as well as words, parents usually can enable the kindergarten child to accept school. If there is parental conflict so that the child is not given the assurance and support he needs by both parents, then his reluctance to come to school may continue.

It is almost always a mistake to overlook a kindergarten child's reluctance to go to school and to do nothing about it. Underlying fears may then remain and the child may have trouble each year, coming to school with increasing fear and panic.

If there is no new baby in the home, yet the child is fearful of leaving the mother and coming to school, it is likely that the mother is using the child emotionally — over-protecting him and clinging to him because she needs him. This mother is one who, as a rule, is not able to establish a satisfactory relationship with her husband. The child becomes her whole life, and his reason for not wanting to leave her is that he senses her desire to cling to him and not let him go.

Such a mother and child are difficult to help. The teacher who can call on the school psychologist for help is fortunate. If a psychologist is not available but the teacher is aware of the meaning of such clinging, perhaps she can be successful in leading the mother to seek expert advice from a child guidance clinic in the community or a private child psychiatrist or psychologist. The sooner these children are helped, the better chance they have to become independent, free individuals.

It is sometimes beneficial to let the mother of a kindergarten child who is fearful of leaving her come to school and stay a while for two or three days. These visits give the child an opportunity to get acquainted with the teacher and the room before leaving the mother. It will give the mother, also, a chance to get acquainted, and it may then be easier for her to leave the child. Her stay at school should not be continued beyond a short time for the first two or three days. Otherwise, the child may want her to stay indefinitely, and the value of her brief visits will be lost. The teacher should explain this situation clearly to the mother, who can then make it clear to the child that her stay in the school is a brief, temporary arrangement and that his teacher will take good care of him.

Even with this arrangement, the kindergarten child may cry when his mother leaves. The teacher can help him best by giving him some toy to hold or by getting some of the children to draw him into their play. Sometimes the teacher can let him do something with her. Any of these plans are better than just leaving the youngster to cry. The teacher should comfort the child and tell him that she will take good care of him, that he will be safe, and that his mother will be safe while he is away from her.

A little child will respond to the teacher who, kind yet firm in her sympathy, helps him feel that he is expected to be in school like the other boys and girls. He will also respond to her assurance that she wants him and needs him at school.

SUMMARY

The child who is fearful of coming to school is, as a rule, not afraid of school per se but is anxious and fearful. When an individual is filled with anxiety, he fastens this concern onto something; these phobic children turn it toward school. If they can be kept in school, they may be helped to overcome this particular fear. If, on the other hand, nothing is done to remove their anxiety, it is then transferred onto something other than school.

For these children to be in school is preferable, however, for they usually get considerable satisfaction from such attendance and it is better for them to be with others than to be alone at home.

It is not always easy for the teacher to help the child with school phobia. When special guidance services are available in the school or community, they should be obtained if possible.

10

Learning Disabilities

There are all degrees of learning disability, ranging from a slight lag in terms of grade norms to serious non-learning with a lag of several years. The child who tests approximately six months below the expected grade score on a standardized achievement test does not have a serious learning problem; the one who tests two or three years below the expected score does have. Pupils with serious learning disabilities usually have difficulty in all school subjects, but at-

tention is directed toward reading since this ability is necessary
for most school learning.

The time has come when schools must recognize *severe*
learning disabilities for what they really are: *symptoms of emotional disturbance or neurotic behavior.* In other words, all
children of normal intelligence — as measured by an individual
intelligence test — can and will learn adequately if they are
emotionally ready to learn and if they have no serious physical
condition, such as a hearing or visual defect. By "adequately"
is meant achieving within the range considered normal for a
particular age level. The pupil with normal intelligence is
capable of achieving at any appropriate grade level, although
he may not achieve much beyond this. If he is in a class with
many children of superior intelligence, he will probably gain
an average of C while the superior students achieve A or B.

A word of caution is advisable in regard to determining
whether a child has "normal" intelligence. This can be reason-
ably decided only if the child is examined by a competent
psychologist. Children who resist learning and present serious
learning problems frequently test low on group intelligence
tests as well as on individual tests if they are emotionally disturbed. Only trained clinicians can determine — on the basis
of several tests — whether or not the child has good or normal
intelligence in these instances.

The statement that "all children of normal intelligence can
learn" assumes, of course, that the child attends school regularly and comes from a home where learning is valued. Some
children in our public schools come from homes where the
parents have little or no education and do not value education
themselves. The children, consequently, may lack the incen-
tive or the interest to learn. Other children, however, whose
parents have had little education, are encouraged to learn and
profit from *all* educational experiences.

Much is said of motivation and its place in learning. Most young children are highly motivated to learn unless they come from a very deprived home; they learn if teaching methods are even moderately adequate. There are certain optimal methods for teaching, and it is advisable to use the best systems for the sake of expediency and efficiency. But children can learn under a variety of methods.

Children seem to learn at various rates of speed, and some seem ready for learning before others. This is logical when we think of individual differences in children and the range of normality in walking or talking, for instance. It seems pretty well established that children should have a mental age of about six and one-half before they are introduced to reading. To delay reading until a child is seven years of age would probably insure a high percentage of success in beginners.

In first grade, when a child is not learning as rapidly as his mother wants him to, or thinks he should, he may become disturbed by his mother's anxiety. He may feel that he has failed and that there is something wrong with him.

The teacher cannot allay a parent's anxiety about her child's "slowness" in starting reading by telling her not to worry. He must show the mother what the child is learning and how he is helping him. He needs, also, to let the mother see that he is alert in giving the child every opportunity to learn without making him feel anxious or pressured. The mother wants to know that the child is not forgotten or pushed aside because he does not seem "ready" for reading when the other children do. This is another function of the teacher, and he can give both the child and the mother immeasurable help. Often, serious reading problems begin with a parent's anxiety. The anxious parent makes the child anxious, and frequently attempts to do something about the reading, only making matters worse. If the mother is secure in the knowledge that the teacher is on the job and if she gets a careful explanation of how her child is being helped, there will be less danger of her doing anything harmful.

Something should be said at this point in recognition of the fact that not all children can be excellent readers or students. We must accept a range of skill in reading as well as in other areas, such as music and art. But, all normal children can learn to read adequately, if not excellently. A child can become disturbed because his parents or teachers are unaccepting of what, for him, is "good" achievement. This is an important point to keep in mind when dealing with so-called "learning disabilities."

If a normal child is not making a pretty good start in learning in the second grade, it is time to be concerned. By this age, children usually have achieved the maturational level essential for formal learning and are highly motivated to learn. In most instances, the reasons for non-learning do not lie within the teaching but within the child. His non-learning is usually a symptom of some emotional disturbance of greater or lesser degree.

We must never jump to conclusions, however, but should have a careful study or appraisal made by a competent school psychologist and a pediatrician. There should be a careful medical examination to rule out any physical causes for the non-learning. Only in rare instances do we find a physical cause for non-learning, but we must be sure. The physical cause can be poor vision or hearing or general poor health making for lack of energy. Many children, however, who have a hearing or visual defect become excellent students, while others who have normal physical senses fail to learn.

An evaluation of the pupil's intellectual level should be made as a further diagnostic process. Many schools of today use group intellegence tests, and while these are usually adequate as an estimate of *mental ability* for children over eight years of age, they are not adequate for the child who is having difficulty in *learning*. An individual intelligence test should be given and interpreted by a competent school psychologist; only then can a reliable opinion of the pupil's mental ability be obtained. Following this examination, a complete personality study should be made by the psychologist so that reasons for the child's non-learning can be obtained. If there are no serious physical or mental defects, the non-learning behavior indicates some emotional conflict which can be discovered by psychological examination.

Non-learning symptoms mean different things for different children. For example, some children fail to learn because they do not want to grow up. By not learning, they think they can remain weak and helpless and in need of the extra care they are asking for. Some children do not learn because it is not worth their while. Their parents have not given them the attention and affection that indicates they are loved and important; therefore, they do not feel it is worthwhile doing something they know the parents want them to do.

Some children unconsciously use non-learning as a weapon to express resentment toward parents. It is an effective weapon and one over which the child maintains complete control. Nobody can make him learn if he does not want to. Often, when a child enters therapy, he becomes aware of the meaning of his school failure and drops this neurotic pattern. The older child who is angry at his parents may use non-learning as a two-edged sword — he punishes his parents and also himself. He feels so guilty because of his resentment toward his parents that he thinks he needs to be punished. He, therefore, fails in his school work and is punished by non-promotion, by the scorn of his classmates, and by the anger and/or punishment of his parents.

Some children fail to learn because they think they must not know certain things. To learn to read is to learn forbidden things, often sexual in nature. So these children become "non-learners." Certain children are just so unhappy and confused because of parental neglect or conflict that they cannot mobilize their energies to learn.

As we see in the above illustrations the reasons why normal children do not learn, it is easy to understand why punishment, extra study, or remedial reading do not as a rule help these children. Many non-learners are seen by adults as compliant, good-natured children who try hard to learn without success. Or, they may be seen as good-natured but lazy, and the adults feel they could learn if they would only try. Children themselves will give many "reasons" why they cannot learn. They say, "It is too hard," or "I am stupid." All of them think they really want to learn, and they suffer from the ridicule of their classmates — which is usually well concealed from the teacher. The child sincerely believes he cannot learn, for the unconscious causes are hidden from him too.

Many of you will recall from your experiences certain children who were helped to read by "extra study" or "remedial help." When this occurs, some change has come into the life of the child that makes it no longer necessary for him to continue non-learning as a neurotic symptom. He learns, therefore, and the "remedial reading" or the "extra study" gets the credit.

Sometimes a remedial reading teacher who is warm and accepting can be therapeutic enough in the approach he uses so that the child will learn. In this case, it is actually the good relationship that is responsible for the child's learning rather than the extra teaching. Some therapists have had little children tell them they will learn for them but for no one else. This happens when the therapist has won the child's love and trust.

When this happens, the youngster learns his daily school lessons with no extra tutoring. Sometimes, a fourth or fifth grade child has missed so much while he was resisting learning that he needs tutoring at the point in his therapy at which he becomes receptive to learning.

Older children often give up their neurotic, non-learning behavior after considerable therapy and become highly motivated to learn. If they have superior intelligence, they may "catch up" without tutoring; if they have average intelligence, they may need special tutoring for a while.

A careful psychological study made on the second grade child who is showing no positive steps toward learning should be followed by therapy if it seems that the child has an emotional disturbance which will keep him from learning. A psychological study is not always easy to have done because of the limited psychological services available to many schools. If and when educators become aware of the meaning of non-learning behavior, they may take the necessary steps to insure this service. It probably would be far more profitable for the schools to have psychologists, able to give therapy to "non-learning" children, than to have a team of remedial teachers. Classroom teachers can be responsible for helping pupils who lag somewhat in reading, but the child who has a serious reading disability needs special help from a trained therapist.

TEACHERS AND NON-LEARNERS

In order to help a non-learner, the teacher needs the benefit of a careful psychological study of the child. Following this study, teacher and psychologist together can plan the best classroom approach. This approach will vary with the individual pupil and with the seriousness of the child's symptoms. Regardless of psychological findings, the teacher can help the non-learner feel he is capable of learning by giving him encouraging support when he is successful, by giving him small amounts of material to master, and by giving him as much warm, personal attention as is possible in the classroom situation.

Teachers of high school pupils who present serious learning disabilities must rely upon psychological help. The high school pupil with normal intelligence who is a non-learner usually needs intensive therapy. His neurotic pattern is so firmly fixed that, without active participation in a therapeutic situation, he goes on failing without knowing why. Furthermore, he usually becomes a non-participant in all school activities. In other words, he may withdraw from all normal contacts, both learning and social.

The pupil who occasionally lags can sometimes be spurred on to greater activity when some teacher or counselor takes a personal interest in him and thereby raises his level of aspiration. Sometimes, when a child gets a taste of real satisfaction from achievement, he continues to achieve well. A pupil who has lagged all through school may become intensely interested in some particular subject in high school and suddenly begin achieving when his interest carries him along. These students can be helped by teachers and counselors through their personal encouragement and interest.

At the high school level, remedial reading can be of benefit if the pupil sees the need for it and if his cooperation is gained. Otherwise, special help can be a waste of time and money. Parents who force tutoring or remedial reading on a high school pupil are approaching the problem in the wrong way. The pupil's cooperation and own wishes must be considered.

When educators realize the seriousness of severe learning disabilities in elementary school children of normal intelligence and are able to do something about this problem, the time may come when high schools will not be faced with such non-learning problems in normally intelligent children. Of course, this will be a tremendous task for the elementary school. It will necessitate having psychological therapists available, either through the schools or the community, to give these children the proper aid. In the meantime, teachers will have to use their ingenuity in trying to interest the child in learning by making it very rewarding to him. They can do this by giving warm praise for every little success and by making the child feel it is worthwhile to please them.

CHILDREN WITH LEARNING DIFFICULTIES

Emily was referred to the school psychologist as a non-learner when she was in fifth grade. She was struggling with second or third grade reading in fifth grade. She was failing spelling and arithmetic. Her papers were almost illegible.

Emily's intelligence was in the superior level as measured by an individual intelligence test. In fact, she had an I.Q. of 135 on a Binet Intelligence Scale. She had been given special individual attention and remedial reading by a reading teacher since she was in first grade. Both Emily and her mother were discouraged. Her mother blamed the school, although the school had provided extensive remedial instruction.

After some review of Emily's history, the psychologist decided to see her weekly for therapy and to recommend no further tutoring or remedial reading. Therapy was carried on weekly for a period of approximately eight months. Emily was told that her time with the psychologist was to be spent in a different way from that spent with the remedial reading teacher. She was told that she was intelligent but that there was something keeping her from learning. She could talk about anything she wanted to in her sessions.

Emily made good use of her time. A voluble ten-year-old, she had no trouble verbalizing her many conflicts with her family and friends. Only once did she mention school work, and at that time she wanted the psychologist to show her how to study her spelling so she could learn words. This done, Emily's spelling marks went from forty to eighty and ninety in two or three weeks' time.

Her greatest source of conflict lay with her mother, and much time was spent in helping Emily understand her feelings in relation to her mother. She also had many sexual confusions and was able to get these answered and clarified.

As Emily's conflicts and confusions were clarified and eliminated, she began to improve in her school work. She had no further tutoring or remedial reading, but went ahead on her own initiative with encouragement from her teacher. By the end of sixth grade, she was achieving well and went on to junior high school where she made a successful adjustment to all classes and achieved excellent marks.

During eight months of therapy, Emily had gone from a school failure to a successful, creative student. She had been using "non-learning" as an unconscious means of defeating her mother, toward whom she was very angry for many reasons. With therapy she worked through these feelings and, in so doing, established a much better relationship with her mother. She now did not need to continue to fail to learn, since the neurotic conflict had been relieved.

George was referred to the psychologist when he was six years old. He was one of the most disorganized, hyperactive, and destructive children the psychologist had ever seen. He made it very difficult for the teacher to work with the group of children in her class, and he did not learn.

In her study of George, the psychologist discovered that his parents had recently been divorced and the father had remarried. The mother, a young woman who saw her whole future ruined, thought it would be impossible to support a child, and contemplated giving him up, either by placing him in an institution or a foster home. George saw the whole world as unsafe and feared personal destruction. No wonder he could not learn, although he had superior intelligence and a wonderful teacher.

Taken on for therapy by the school psychologist, he was seen weekly for about two and one-half years. At the end of the first grade he had made no perceptible beginning in learning, but he was calmer and a little less confused and frightened. His mother was seen at intervals by the psychologist, who tried to help her reorganize her life and her plans for George.

George went on to second grade where he had another warm and supportive teacher. He continued in therapy all this year. At the end of the second grade he had made marked gains in learning but was still reading only on a beginning first grade level.

In third grade he again was fortunate in having a warm, accepting teacher. The psychologist continued to see him almost weekly for that year too. He had become a relatively calm, organized youngster, although his home life was still quite insecure. At the end of third grade he tested at fourth grade level in reading; his number concepts and writing were also good.

Because this boy received therapy and had three excellent teachers who were supportive, accepting, and warm, he was able to learn. Without this help he would unquestionably have continued to be a non-learner. He had no remedial reading or tutoring of any kind, and it is almost certain that he would have been unable to respond to it in the beginning. Later he did not need it.

He was too frightened to learn much in first and second grade. He did not know who would take care of him or who really wanted him, and the whole world was a potentially dangerous place. He was so frightened that, if a custodian mowing the lawn came near the therapy room, he would pale visibly and ask for reassurance from the psychologist that he was safe.

The psychologist and his teachers helped him see that he was loved and wanted and that he would be taken care of. His mother gradually worked out some solution to her problems so she could give him more stability in his home life.

The psychologist and the teachers constantly praised George to his mother and helped her see what a capable, attractive boy he was. They dwelt only on his assets, his strong points, and his need for security in their talks with the mother. This was an important approach because the mother felt so rejected herself that any adverse criticism of the child would only mean further rejection and discouragement for her.

Because of the school's approach, George became a fairly well-integrated child who was successful in learning and in his social relations with others. If the school had been unable to help George, he would have remained a disturbed "non-learner."

Implications for schools in this point of view toward non-learners in the elementary school are far-reaching. They would cause changes to be made in remedial reading, in screening children with learning disabilities, and in the attitude toward promotion versus non-promotion. For example, any child of seven not making healthy strides in formal learning would be given a careful psychological evaluation. This psychological evaluation would determine the reasons for the non-learning behavior, and steps could be taken to treat the child to remove his emotional conflicts. His energies would then be released for learning.

As a rule, no child would be asked to "repeat" a grade because he had not learned to read. Sound psychological reasons for this should be self-evident in the light of our discussion on non-learners. Repeating a grade will usually intensify the child's neurotic feelings and make it even harder to help him.

Sometimes it seems necessary to ask a "non-learner" to repeat a grade because it is difficult to give him the individualized instruction he requires to stay with his age mates. This is sometimes true in a public school where the classes are larger. Such a poor solution, however, usually has harmful effects on the child. It is far better for him to go on and to receive psychological therapy so he can be freed of his neurotic symptoms.

SUMMARY

In conclusion, the premise here presented is this: *All normal children can and do learn.* When they do not learn, we must see the non-learning as a form of "poor adjustment" to life situations. Instead of advocating more study, tutoring, non-promotion, or punishment, we must provide psychological diagnosis and treatment just as we do when a child presents other symptoms of "poor adjustment" or neurotic behavior.

Remedial assistance or special reading help would be supplied in instances where it seemed fitting. If the psychological study indicated that the child was ready to respond to special help and needed it, then such assistance could be supplied.

This premise takes us away from a mechanistic point of view to a dynamic one. It helps us see children, not as objects we "do things to" or manipulate, but as human beings who need help in working through solutions to deep personal problems. We can provide this help through psychological counseling or therapy.

11

Truancy

Truancy from school can mean one of two things: the pupil is escaping from an intolerable situation in which the school program brings him nothing but failure, shame, disgrace, and ridicule from his peers, or the pupil is suffering from serious emotional conflict. In either event, truancy is a symptom demanding immediate attention from responsible adults.

To determine the reasons for truancy, a careful study should be made of the pupil by the school authorities and the psychologist. Since truancy indicates desperateness on the part of the child, all the forces in the home, the school, and the community should be marshalled to help if they are needed. Schools have the responsibility of seeing that every pupil is provided a program wherein his needs are met, and of calling an emotionally disturbed child to the attention of the proper individuals. Schools can foster truancy and juvenile delinquency as well as emotional illness by failing or refusing to recognize their responsibility in regard to the truant pupil.

Teachers play an important role in being alert to distress signals warning of possible truancy in a pupil. Some of these signals have been discussed earlier but will be mentioned again. Any child who fails to make a good adjustment to school life is a potential truant. If he constantly meets failure or is unable to get along with his peers, we should be warned that the child is in distress. If the child aligns himself with the "fringers" in the community or with other children who feel unaccepted by the group and who take part in anti-social mischief or pranks, then we should be alert.

The teacher should be aware of children who are frequently absent for vague reasons or minor ailments. This pattern usually indicates an unhappy child—one who does not feel identified with his school group—and sometimes forewarns of the later truant. If the teacher notices a child having frequent absences, he can confer with the parents and the school psychologist. Together they may be able to discover the child's reasons for finding it difficult to come to school and plan ways to help him.

It is always easier to help a disturbed child when the early warning signals are noted than to wait until he is deeply involved in trouble and emotional conflicts. If we fail to heed early signs and the pupil becomes a chronic truant, the youngster's feelings about himself and others will have become crystallized to a degree where it will be more difficult to help him.

By this time, he feels so unwanted and so bitter against people that it will take a long time to change his feelings and attitudes. Here are several brief case histories of children who became truants.

Jock was one of two children living in an upper middle-class family in a community of high economic level. The parents were well educated, serious-minded people with strong religious beliefs. The father was older than the mother and was the stricter of the two in his religious and moral scruples. He constantly held the children to extremely difficult standards which they could not meet. Because they failed to meet his expectations, they became discouraged and depressed. They also became filled with angry and resentful feelings toward the parents who made them feel so inadequate. Both children were bright, but they did poor work in school as a result of their feelings of inadequacy.

The boy, the older of the two children, was made to repeat a grade because he did not read as well as his teachers thought he should. This was a terrible blow to the sensitive child and intensified his feelings of depression and resentment. He began to withdraw from school and neighborhood activities the year he repeated fourth grade. He pulled off into fantasy which made him "absent-minded," and his school work continued to suffer. He became so self-conscious with other children that he would forget to uphold his end on a committee. He was called irresponsible by both teacher and children.

Jock's "truancy" began with frequent illnesses of a minor nature that kept him out of school for a day or two at a time. As he became more agitated, he found it increasingly difficult to come to school. Finally, the day came when he refused to come to school and became hysterical when his mother insisted. He threatened to run away or to kill himself if she forced him to go to school. The mother concealed the truancy from the father and the school for a short while on the excuse of illness. She gradually began to realize the seriousness of Jock's disturbance and sought advice from a psychologist in private practice.

The psychologist, realizing the acuteness of Jock's distress and anxiety, took steps to get him into treatment. She recommended that the mother place him in a small private school until he was able to respond to treatment enough to make progress in his school work. Under treatment, he was relieved of his anxiety and was able to "catch up" in the work he had missed while so upset. At the end of two years, Jock was able to return to the public school and take his place in a group of children his own age.

William was a boy who received special help through the school. He lived at the edge of an upper-income bracket community with his grandparents and his mother. The grandparents were hard-working people. The mother was a weak, emotionally ill individual who escaped from her troubles through drink. William's father "just wasn't around," and it is doubtful if the mother had ever married.

Because of William's home and his mother's neglect due to her own problems and incapacity, William was a "fringer" in school. He felt he was an outsider, and, although he had normal intelligence, he was so depressed that he failed to learn. He attended a school where classes were large and where the teachers had no time to give him any attention. Consequently, when he did not learn, he was pushed to the back of the class and forgotten.

School became intolerable for William and he became intolerable to the teachers. He became a truant at the age of nine and stayed away from school days at a time. Finally, when he had been truant for about three weeks in succession, the school investigated his absences. The grandparents and the mother had assumed William was in school because he left each morning and returned each afternoon when school was over.

As a result of this experience, William was entered in a public school where the classes were smaller and the teachers had time to help him. He began to like school a little better as his teacher, the psychologist, and the shop instructor took an interest in him and showed concern about what he did. The psychologist saw him for weekly counseling sessions over a period of several months. His teacher established a good relationship with him and invited him to come for special help so that he could catch up on his work. Since William was handy with tools and enjoyed working in the shop, the shop instructor let him come and work there whenever he had the time. William's truancy ended, and he began to take more of an interest in learning. He remained basically depressed because of the home situation over which the school had no control.

When he was ready for junior high school, William was placed in the special class program for slow learners so that he could have the individual help and guidance of the special class teacher. His academic work was on a low level although he had average intelligence. Rather than have him meet failure again, he was assigned to the special class for academic subjects and attended gym, music, shop, and art with the regular classes.

William was saved from a life of delinquency and truancy through the help of the school. He was aided to achieve success in his work on the level at which he was able to function. If he had received the proper attention from the school at an earlier age, he might have been more successful in his school learning and have been less depressed and fearful of life. School might have been one area of his life where he received acceptance and constructive attention from the beginning.

Sara was fourteen and in junior high school when she was

referred to the psychologist for help. She lived in a lower middle-class family in a high-income community. Her mother died when she was about twelve years old, leaving the father with Sara and two older boys.

The loss of her mother left Sara without anyone who really cared what happened to her. The father, a busy, hard-working man, had little affection for Sara and knew nothing about taking care of an adolescent daughter. Sara's clothes were not in good taste, and she soon found herself on the edge of all social activities in her class and community. She did have some social life with one or two girls who felt sorry for her, but they did not really like her.

Although Sara was not a brilliant student, she was capable of doing passing work. After her mother's death, however, she began to fail in her school subjects and to become more and more disinterested in school. She felt quite "out of things" as the other girls ostracized her from their social grouping and parties.

Since there was no one at home who cared when she got to school or when she came home, she began coming to school tardy, then gradually became a truant. She stayed out late at night and began associating with a few other community "fringers" who met at soda fountains and the corner drug store. When her school attendance became poor and her marks were failures, she was referred to the school psychologist for assistance.

The psychologist made a careful study of the entire situation and thoroughly evaluated the possibility of giving Sara the assistance and the supervision a young adolescent needs from her family. The father seemed either unable or uninterested in providing a motherly housekeeper, and it became necessary to find a good boarding school for Sara. The psychologist worked with the father to help him locate a school and obtain the necessary financial assistance he needed to pay for it. This was done through the Child Welfare Department of the Children's Court. While plans were being made, the psychologist worked with Sara to help her accept living away from home. Sara was not completely satisfied with the new arrangement, but accepted it as a better solution than the unbearable home and school situation.

Although it is always better from the standpoint of the pupil to try to work out solutions on home ground, it is not always possible to do so. Then, the responsible adults have to take steps to work out the next best solution. The teacher who can plan her program so that all children feel the satisfaction of achievement, regardless of their abilities, will do much to prevent delinquency. It is not always the school that the truant is running away from, however. If the teacher cannot help the child *want* to come to school, the home situation must be explored. Many times it is the home the child is trying to run away from. Unhappy in the home, he is too depressed to face school and his classmates. If this is true, the teacher will need the assistance of the school psychologist or social worker in helping the child.

SUMMARY

Truancy is usually symptomatic of a serious personality disturbance and should receive prompt, thoughtful attention. Too often, truancy is treated purely as a disciplinary matter. Children making a normal adjustment to life do not wish to isolate themselves from their peers and run away from school life. While disciplinary action may be necessary as a first step toward getting the pupil back into regular attendance, it should be seen as an emergency measure. The pupil should receive the assistance of the school psychologist and other interested personnel so that he can be helped to attain a better emotional adjustment.

12

Stuttering and Other Speech Problems as Symptoms

Speech is a part of the total personality, just as are good nature, patience, or ill temper. The individual's manner of speaking gives a picture of his feelings about himself— self-concept—and the way he expects others to respond to him. Change an individual's self-concept and you change his speech. If he feels confident, his tones convey this feeling. If he is discouraged, his voice tells you so. If he feels others reject him, he may either try to force acceptance of his ideas by loud, emphatic speech or speak in a hesitating manner because he feels he has nothing worthy of your attention.

A child's personality is taking shape as he has experiences with parents and friends. His speech is a clue as to what is happening to him in these personal relationships. Stuttering, then, seen as a projection of the individual's self-concept, indicates that the child is suffering deep feelings of conflict in his personal relations with others. These conflicts stem from parent-child relations, and most frequently from the mother-child relationship.

If you will recall from earlier chapters the statements in regard to a child's need for a consistent, secure relationship with his parents, you will understand the nature of the conflicts causing stuttering. The mother, who is usually the source of this difficulty, is always a person having many unresolved emotional problems of her own. These unresolved problems make her anxious; in managing her anxiety she finds it necessary to attempt to control her environment, which includes her husband and her children. Attempts to control her environment are necessary to relieve her anxiety. If one can "keep things under control," one is less anxious.

Such a controlling mother causes her child excessive frustration. She also binds him to her in an extreme dependency relationship. When someone is constantly telling you what to do or demanding that you cease certain behavior, you reach the state where you dare not use your own initiative. The stuttering child is usually passive and submissive, and rarely uses his own initiative. His dependency is prolonged because his mother has made him fearful of using his own wits. She has usually made him feel weak, inadequate, and unsatisfactory because he can never be as good and compliant as she wishes him to be.

Along with this strong dependency are the concomitant emotions of resentment and rebellion. These emotions are usually deeply repressed in the unconscious. All children need the mother's acceptance and good will, and they repress rebellious feelings if they are afraid to express them. Repression of these deeply rebellious and angry feelings causes the stuttering. The child is afraid to express them, yet they are there. The unconscious fear that he will utter them and thus lose his mother's needed approval makes him stutter.

Stuttering, therefore, should be a signal to the teacher that the child is caught up in this dependency-rebellious relationship with all the angry, hostile feelings that go along with it. The child is usually quite unaware of his true feelings because they are so carefully repressed. He is often amazed in a therapeutic setting when these feelings begin to come to the surface.

The mother, too, is surprised at the nature of the child's feelings and often cannot accept them as being valid. She also finds it difficult—or even impossible—to recognize the part she plays in keeping the child dependent upon her. She protests that she does not like him to be so dependent and becomes annoyed at the restriction his dependency places upon her. All the time, however, she is unconsciously fostering and prolonging the dependency and the buried hostility.

This, in brief, is the cause of stuttering, although the description is greatly over-simplified. Complex and complicated ramifications enter into each specific instance, but it does not seem essential for our purpose to elaborate them in greater detail.

Here, we must discuss what can be done to help the child. Obviously, both mother and child need treatment, since the stuttering indicates the presence of emotional problems in the lives of each. The problems are interrelated, and the young child's improvement depends upon the mother's.

If the child is under school age, his speech often clears up if the mother is helped to work out some of her problems. In the school age child, both parent and child need treatment.

With or without treatment, there are several things the school can do. *The stuttering must be overlooked and given no direct attention.* When direct attention is drawn to the speech, the child becomes more conscious of it. He also becomes more tense and hostile. It makes him feel as though he is being criticized for something over which he has no control and gives him further evidence that he is not satisfactory to his parents and teachers. Since the reason for the stuttering is psychological, calling attention to it by asking the child to slow down or by giving him speech lessons is futile. This point of view is not always accepted by speech specialists, some of whom feel that the stutterer can be "trained to speak correctly." However, one cannot help a child overcome his emotional problems or change his self-concept through "speech training."

The speech, then, should be overlooked by the school and the parents. When the stuttering is severe, this becomes a difficult task, for it is often painful to the listener to hear and watch. It makes the listener feel he should do something to help. The best help is to try to listen quietly and supply the word the child is stumbling over when the hesitation is unduly prolonged.

The school can aid this child in all the ways one helps a child feel wanted and adequate. The more secure he feels, the less he will stutter. It is not uncommon to find a child stuttering severely at home and not at all in school, when he is made to feel accepted and successful in the latter place.

Sometimes a child's conflicts in the home become so intense, and his anger and frustration so severe, that his speech becomes almost paralyzed. When this occurs, the teacher should not call upon him to read orally or to recite before the class. He can talk to the child confidentially and relieve him of the fear that he will be called on and tell him he can volunteer when he feels comfortable. This will remove the youngster's intense fear of being called on during the acute period of stuttering. If he is not embarrassed at school, he will soon feel free again to contribute to classroom discussions, and the acute period may soon pass.

Stutterers are often able to sing and take part in plays without stuttering. They should be permitted to take part in as many activities as they wish to and are able to participate in successfully. All stutterers, together with their mothers, should receive psychiatric treatment. Sometimes the school psychologist can induce the parents to take this step if treatment facilities are available in the community. If they are not available, then anything the home and the school can do to relieve pressures and tensions and make the child feel secure and accepted will be beneficial.

Often a young child is labeled a stutterer when he is *not* one. This comes about when he shows some hesitation or repetition in his speech during an exciting or stressful situation. *Ignoring the hesitation* and making sure that the young child feels secure and receives sufficient rest if the hesitation recurs or persists is the best procedure. This procedure will ordinarily cause it to disappear unless it symbolizes a deep disturbance. If attention is given to the speech, the pattern may become fixated as the child becomes uncomfortable and self-conscious about it. Sometimes a child gives up stuttering and takes on another symptom, such as a tic, nail-biting, or obsessive actions and thoughts. This phenomenon is further evidence that stuttering is psychological in origin and cannot be benefited by speech correction or training.

After a child has received psychotherapy and his emotional conflicts have been resolved, his speech usually clears up spontaneously. Sometimes the older child can profit from some speech training when his emotional conflicts have been relieved. He may feel the speech training will be helpful and he can at this time derive benefit from it with a skilled speech specialist. Speech lessons should never be instituted, however, without the advice of the psychiatrist or psychologist who is treating the child.

At this point, a few illustrations of children who stuttered will make the preceding discussion more graphic.

Mary was four-and-a-half when her mother came to see the school psychologist. Although not yet in school, she would be entering kindergarten in the fall of the next year. Her mother was eager to have some help so that Mary would not be teased in school about her speech. A stutterer, she had been afflicted with the difficulty for several months.

The psychologist and the principal agreed that Mary and her mother should be given help, even though Mary was not yet in school. A history obtained from the mother brought the following pertinent information. Mary was the youngest of three children, there being an older sister and brother. Greatly loved by her parents and the many relatives who lived near, she was given so much attention that she was constantly over-stimulated and never permitted to play quietly by herself or with children of her own age. She was actually the "play-thing" of the adoring parents and relatives who constantly exploited her by asking her to perform or show off in some way. It was not easy to see why Mary was given so much attention when there were two other children in the home. She was, however, an attractive, gay, alert little girl who responded to this attention in a way evidently very satisfying to the adults.

As a result of the great attention given Mary, the older sister became very jealous of her and used to tease her unmercifully. The two girls slept together and this gave the sister further opportunity to tease little Mary. Most unhappy about this teasing, Mary dreaded going to bed at night. She did not get the rest a child her age needed.

Because Mary seemed so precocious, she was permitted to

take part in activities similar to the older sister's. For example, she was allowed to go to a neighborhood roller-skating rink where she took part in skating lessons and exhibitions. Her skill and petiteness charmed the adults who applauded this skill heartily.

As the psychologist talked to the mother, she realized that Mary was being pushed beyond the limits any four-year-old should be asked to achieve. Never allowed to be a little girl, she was always on display. Without realizing it, the parents were frustrating Mary by not letting her be a little girl with a little girl's interests. They were expecting her to be a source of pleasure to them and were expecting her to be too grownup.

In her play therapy sessions, Mary played out the little girl whose mother sent her up to bed alone and showed how lonesome she was. She also played out the anger toward the parent who pushed her too hard and toward the big sister who teased her.

The mother began to see what she had unconsciously or unwittingly been doing to Mary, and took immediate steps to change many things. She provided a separate bedroom for Mary. She took the time to go with Mary to her bedroom at night and to sit with her, either reading a story or just sitting quietly. She stopped the older sister's teasing and gave her an equal share of attention.

The psychologist advised that Mary be removed from the over-stimulation of the skating-rink, with its skating lessons and exhibitions. She also advised the mother to stop asking Mary to perform for adults, whether it be singing, dancing, or reciting nursery rhymes. The mother was able to gain the cooperation of the relatives, and this exploitation ceased.

As the mother made the changes described and as Mary played out her feelings of resentment and unhappiness, her stuttering lessened and gradually disappeared altogether. Mary entered kindergarten the following fall, and a follow-up of her for several years showed no recurrence of the speech difficulty. She was a happy, intelligent little girl who made a good adjustment to school, both academically and socially.

Because Mary's mother was basically a fairly well-adjusted person herself, she was able to make changes necessary to help Mary. Through her talks with the psychologist and her ability to alter the factors contributing to Mary's tension and stuttering, she actually took part in the therapy herself. Had the mother been less well-adjusted and had she been unable to work along with the psychologist, it is doubtful if Mary could have made such a satisfactory and apparently permanent recovery.

It is only fair to give a report of a stutterer who was not so easily or successfully helped. Failure occurred because the parents were deeply neurotic and proved unable to change their attitude toward the child.

Sam was an only child. His father was basically a weak man with many eccentric qualities; the mother—dependent, anxious, and controlling—remained completely unconscious of her part in Sam's problems. Sam saw his father as a man whose "bark was worse than his bite." He saw his mother as "stern, unyielding, demanding, and controlling." He felt—and rightly so —that neither parent understood him.

His stuttering began just before he went to kindergarten. The school psychologist conferred with the parents and they agreed to obtain treatment for Sam, but treatment was discontinued after a few short months because the mother could not let anyone but herself control Sam.

Sam went along in school and was given training by a speech specialist for at least two years. In fourth grade his teacher asked for help through the school psychologist. At this time Sam's stuttering was extremely severe, and he was quite with-

drawn from classroom participation. The psychologist conferred with the parents, who professed to be interested in
helping Sam. They asked for help through the school.

Speech training was discontinued and Sam entered treatment
with the psychologist. He was then nine and one-half years
of age and had been stuttering for four or five years. Therapy
was continued for almost two years. Sam became less tense;
he was able to talk to the psychologist without stuttering. He
began to make friends, to participate in classroom activities,
and to be far less inhibited as a person. The children, who had
previously left him strictly alone, became friendly and said,
"Sam is a good guy."

There were times when he did not stutter in the classroom;
then, when things were bad at home, he would stutter for a
time. The parents were completely unable to alter their attitudes and unconsciously resisted treatment for Sam. They
still felt they wanted him to be helped, but their actions belied
this expressed desire.

Sam obtained considerable insight into the reasons for his
stuttering and was able to rid himself of many repressed feelings of anger and resentment toward his parents. He was,
however, too dependent on them to be able to go all the way
in treatment, and so success was only partial.

When he went to junior high school, he discussed with the
psychologist his wishes in connection with further therapy.
Sam decided against it for the time being. He further asked
that he not be requested to have any more speech training,
should his stuttering recur with any degree of severity in high
school. This request, naturally, was carried out; the speech
training had been discontinued when therapy was begun.

Sam continued to stutter with greater or less intensity in
junior high school. He accepted it, though, and understood the
reasons for it. He did not let the stuttering interfere with his

school work or activities. Some day, when Sam gets older, he may ask for therapy on his own initiative and be cured completely of his stuttering.

This story of Sam illustrates the need for the parents—especially the mother—to take an active part in the therapeutic process with a young child. The improvement of the young child is contingent upon the mother's ability to alter her attitudes and feelings in relation to him.

Some children show emotional disturbances through other forms of speech disorders. The seriously disturbed child—the schizophrenic one—may not talk at all or may talk in such garbled language that he cannot be understood. This kind of speech is often wrongly diagnosed. The child is suspected of not hearing adequately and may be given speech training as a remedial measure. This, of course, is not effective. If a schizophrenic child responds to psychotherapy, his speech will improve spontaneously in most instances. Sometimes speech lessons are beneficial when the child has improved enough through therapy to be able to cooperate willingly.

Some children have "baby talk" prolonged by the parents who think it is cute. This is not the child's problem, but the parents'. The child will speak correctly when he no longer receives attention through baby talk. Other children talk baby talk—sometimes called letter-substitution—because they do not want to grow up. It seems better to them to remain small and helpless so they can be taken care of. When helped through psychotherapy to overcome their fear of growing up, their speech improves.

One little boy was so neglected by his mother, who was disturbed over her own problems, that he did not talk until late. When he did talk, he could not be understood. His mother never paid any attention to him, nor did she ever talk or read to him. When he was still speaking unintelligibly in first grade and seemed continually depressed, the teacher and parent consulted the school psychologist. The mother was advised to seek counseling for herself to help work out her personal problems. She was further advised to begin spending time with her son and, especially, to hold him on her lap while she read and talked to him. The mother was able to follow this advice, and the little boy came out of his depression. He began playing with other children and became happy in school. His speech improved rapidly, and by third grade, scarcely a trace of the baby talk remained.

In this instance the school speech specialist worked with the boy, also, and, since she made her time with him fun, he enjoyed it. The help he received was largely due to the attention of another kindly adult. When a child is starved for adult attention and love, he reaches out for it. The speech lessons were a time when a kindly adult talked to him and played with him. It was, therefore, beneficial in helping him feel more accepted and important. It is doubtful, however, if the speech lessons alone would have been sufficient to cause the great improvement; this was due to the mother's changed relationship to him and her ability to give him more of herself.

Sometimes children cannot hear correctly and, therefore, mispronounce words. A hearing test will determine whether or not the hearing loss is severe enough to keep the child from getting accurate sounds. Naturally, a hard-of-hearing child may need special speech training. Loss of hearing may also cause emotional problems if the loss is a serious one and the child is shut out from normal conversation. If emotional problems arise, the child should receive psychological help in learning to adjust to his handicap.

Mention should be made here of certain speech idiosyncrasies developed through imitation. Children whose parents have poor speech or strange accents unconsciously adopt these speech patterns. Such a speech pattern can be overcome only by conscious effort on the part of the child when he is old enough and sufficiently interested to cooperate with the teacher or speech specialist. Even then, in moments of excitement and stress, he may lapse into his original speech patterns.

SUMMARY

To summarize the point of view presented, all speech symptoms—with the exception of those noted—should be seen as a reflection of the child's emotional relationships with others and his image of himself as a person. The child's speech will improve as his self-concept improves and as his relationships with others are bettered.

13

Other Symptoms and Their Meaning

TANTRUMS

There are two types of tantrums: the mild and the violent. Usually, the mild kind indicates that the child has found it effective in getting his own way. His parents find it hard to say "No" to any of his demands and give in quickly to a show of temper or anger. These children will, as a rule, respond rapidly to the teacher who is firm and consistent, yet affectionate. It is the kind of behavior which usually disappears when the child learns that it is not effective in swaying adults.

The violent type of tantrum indicates that the child is really disturbed, and, if this behavior recurs over a period of time, it should be seen as a warning to adults that the child is in need of help. The child who has violent tantrums is suffering an acute, if temporary, emotional explosion or upheaval. Momentarily, he becomes completely irrational, blind and deaf to the restraining words or actions of the people around him. A child in a violent tantrum is capable of harming others or himself. He is often angry both at others and himself; at others for their "unfair" behavior toward him, and at himself for his "bad behavior" in failing to please the adults. This child will deny that he is angry at himself, but his behavior belies this denial. When he bangs his head on the floor or destroys some of his own property, he is certainly angry at himself and punishing himself.

The child showing this behavior is one who has been denied consistent understanding, love, and support from his parents. Very confused, he does not know what he can expect from them, nor is he sure what they expect from him. He feels that he can never get from them what he needs or be able to please them and is, therefore, in a constant state of frustration and uncertainty. The wild tantrums indicate his degree of frustration and anger, some of which is directed toward himself. Made to believe that he is bad and unworthy because he constantly fails to please his parents, he feels a need to be punished and does so by banging his head or destroying his property.

Such a child needs immediate help when such tantrum behavior recurs frequently and with violence. In school he must be restrained firmly and matter-of-factly by the teacher. He cannot be allowed to injure others or himself. A small child can be restrained by a woman teacher. In elementary school, the child may be too strong for a woman to restrain and may require a man to help him maintain control. The child should be removed from the group and allowed to recover from the tantrum. When quiet, he should be permitted to re-enter the group and should be comforted by the teacher. He should be told that the teacher likes him and will take care of him. This is important because he will feel frightened after his outburst.

The teacher must persist in his attitude, for it will take the child a long time to learn to trust him and realize he is "fair" to everyone. The parents have been so inconsistent that the child has construed their behavior as being "unfair" to him, and he sees all adults as rejecting and lacking in understanding. The teacher will need to build a good relationship with this child.

The teacher should go even beyond the steps described above. He should refer the child to the school psychologist if one is available. Either the teacher or the psychologist should work with the parents to help them see the child's need for assistance. If there is no psychologist in the school, perhaps the teacher can lead the mother to seek consultation from either some community guidance center or a private source.

Sometimes elementary school teachers who understand the meaning of violent tantrums can help the parents comprehend the situation and change their relationship to the child. This requires time, and some teachers do not have the opportunity to hold frequent conferences with parents while trying to help them see the meaning of the child's behavior.

Occasionally, an older child in the junior or senior high school will have a violent tantrum; such an occurrence must always be considered serious enough to warrant investigation. The older child in a tantrum usually strikes out at others or destroys property. If these rages recur frequently, the youngster is seriously disturbed, and either the school or the community resources should be used to help him. If the school authorities can help him control his tantrums by setting strong limits, he can be maintained in school. However, if he is unable to control his behavior when strong limits are set, he may need to be excluded from school until he has received treatment to clear up his emotional disturbance.

The length of time needed for such treatment will depend upon the nature of the pupil's emotional problems and his responsiveness to treatment. Some children respond quickly while others require a longer time. It takes much longer to help an adolescent than a young child because the adolescent has carried his conflicts over a longer period of time. His feelings of anger and fear toward others are so deep-seated that prolonged treatment and continued good experiences with others are necessary to help him change his attitudes. He believes that others reject him and that he is unworthy of their acceptance.

We should remember that the child who has wild and violent temper tantrums is a disturbed one; basically, he is deeply angry and fearful. There is as much fear as anger in the behavior. Such a child needs help and understanding, not punishment.

An illustration of a child showing mild tantrums is that of *Beth*, a six-year-old. She was an only child and an only grandchild. Consequently, she had been "spoiled" by the adults, who were lavish with their attention and who catered to most of her whims.

When Beth came to first grade, she found it hard to be one of the group. She wanted more than her share of the teacher's attention and would have a mild tantrum when she was expected to follow group plans. The teacher was able to help Beth overcome her tantrums by giving her as much individual attention as she could and by being firm and consistent in her expectations. When Beth found she did not get her own way by having tantrums and that the teacher was affectionate and kindly, as well as firm, she gradually stopped her tantrums. Before the end of the first grade they had disappeared altogether. Beth was achieving satisfaction from being one of the group and from receiving the teacher's praise and approval.

Sara, also six, had violent tantrums which would come on without apparent provocation. She would suddenly strike another child and cry and scream violently. She would strike the teacher, kick her, or clutch her wildly when the teacher went to her to keep her from hurting others. The teacher found it impossible to cope with Sara's violent tantrums and had to call for help through the school office. The principal or his assistant would come and carry the crying, screaming child out of the room to a place where she could calm down.

Sara was the second of two children, having an older brother who was the parents' favorite. The mother was an anxious person who was finding it hard to work out her own life. She was also very dependent, and, like most extremely dependent individuals, she had considerable hidden resentment toward others. Because of her own problems, she found it impossible to give Sara the consistent, steady affection and support she needed. She permitted the older brother to tease Sara, who, in turn, became convinced that her mother did not love her since she permitted the teasing.

The mother resented Sara's demands for attention, although she was permitting Sara's tantrums to rule her. The tantrums were symptomatic of Sara's deep feelings of frustration and rejection. The mother and child were bound together in a terrific struggle, the child trying to get her mother's love and support, the mother angry at her child's demands and embarrassing behavior.

At six, Sara felt no one could be trusted and that no one would really care for her or be fair to her. Her outburst in the classroom came when she thought some child was taking advantage of her as her brother did at home or when she felt the teacher was being partial to others. The teacher had to constantly reassure Sara that she loved her and would take good care of her. Careful to meet Sara's anger with calmness, she showed no anger on her part. Sara was already fearful, and the teacher's anger would have made her more afraid and less able to control her behavior.

It was necessary for Sara to receive therapy and for the mother to have some counseling before the child's unhappiness could be banished and the mother could change her attitude toward her. The mother could not change her attitude and give Sara what she needed until she worked out some of her own problems that got in the way.

Sara made a happy adjustment to school before her conflict with her mother had been solved. This was because she found her teachers to be loving, understanding adults; school became a place where she received great satisfaction. Gradually her relationship with her mother improved, and the tantrums at home disappeared too. This was not until mother and child had received considerable therapy and counseling over a period of two or three years.

CLOWNING BEHAVIOR

The class clown is the child who sees himself as silly and ridiculous; therefore, he acts that way. All behavior expresses an individual's feelings about himself. It is true that the child may get attention from others—he may make others laugh—but the habitual clown is not happy. The clowning behavior is partly an attempt to get attention because he feels he can get recognition in no other way.

Teachers should see the class clown as a child who needs help in changing his self-concept. He needs to begin to see himself as a capable, worthy class member. He needs to have respect for himself and to feel that others respect him. If we can study the class clown and discover some worthy asset or trait to use in building his self-respect and in helping others see him with different eyes, we can change his self-concept. If we can do this, the clowning actions will gradually disappear. When he no longer feels silly and ridiculous, he ceases acting in that fashion.

One should not scold the class clown but should see what he needs and help him. Frequently the teacher needs to obtain the parents' understanding and cooperation in giving the youngster sufficient help. Otherwise, the parents may unwittingly tear down or impede the teacher's plan of action.

ENURESIS

Enuresis is a symptom of emotional disturbance which does not usually come to a teacher's attention. It is being mentioned, however, because a mother sometimes wants to discuss the problem with the teacher when she comes for a conference. Enuresis—inability to control urination—can be both diurnal and nocturnal. If the child wets during the day at school, it then becomes a problem for the teacher. Bed-wetting comes to the teacher's attention only through the mother's information or when the odor of urine is present in the child's clothing.

Parents usually look for a physical basis for the enuresis, but, in almost every instance, the cause is psychological. If a child of six or over is enuretic, he is disturbed. He usually feels neglected by his mother. She may love him, but her own problems or her many duties in connection with the care of the house and the other children may get in the way of her showing it.

Scolding the child or shaming him for the wetting is of no avail. If the symptom is recognized for what it is and if the parents can give the child the security that he needs, the disorder clears up. Such a cure is not always easy to accomplish. Parents are usually unaware of their part in the causation of the child's symptom, and are often unable to change their attitudes. In any event, the wetting should be overlooked, and the child should be given praise when he has a dry night.

If the teacher becomes aware of the symptom, he can help the parent understand its meaning. He may also advise the parent to obtain psychological help for the child. He can help the parent see that limiting liquids, punishing, or offering rewards will not be successful.

Occasionally, enuresis is only one of the symptoms presented by the disturbed child. A complete picture of the child's adjustment can help determine how disturbed he is and how easily he may be able to respond to changes made by the parents. If a child shows a number of symptoms along with the bed-wetting, such as stuttering, poor learning in school, and excessively withdrawn or aggressive behavior, he is seriously disturbed and in need of treatment.

Sometimes a child may seem quite well adjusted except for the bed-wetting. If this begins to taper off between six and seven and then disappears altogether without becoming a source of conflict between parent and child, the child is probably working things out through his daily living.

NERVOUSNESS

The term "nervousness" is a catch-all phrase used to describe the jittery, hyperactive child. When this word is used, it means that the child's behavior is not understood. If the teacher has a "nervous" child in her classroom, he should try to obtain a careful physical and psychological study. The "nervousness" may be caused by either physical or psychological factors, or both.

The tense, anxious, unhappy child often appears nervous, and may develop facial twitches or random body movements. He may become extremely hyperactive and find it impossible to sit still. The source of the anxiety must be found and removed if the child is to overcome his "nervousness."

The fatigued or ill child may become nervous, and only a thorough physical examination will determine if this is the cause. Poor nutrition, eyestrain, or a hearing defect also may cause the child to appear nervous. Sometimes a combination of physical and psychological factors causes the "nervousness"; then, both medical and psychological treatment are necessary.

The teacher's role in connection with the nervous child is to help remove unnecessary pressures from him and call the "nervousness" to the attention of the proper authorities—the parent first, then the school physician and psychologist. Sometimes, after the teacher has discussed the child's "nervousness" with the parent, the latter wishes to consult her own pediatrician or a private psychologist. In fact, she may have done so already. In this case, the teacher can be guided in his approach to the child by the advice of these specialists through the mother.

JEALOUSY

All children are jealous at certain times. Since jealousy is a normal human emotion, it must be faced. We must help children learn to control it without letting it overcome them.

In school, teachers see the effects of jealousy in the young child who does not want to come to school and leave his baby sister or brother at home with the mother. They see the jealousy toward other children when a little child wants to have all the teacher's attention and does not want to share it with others. The classroom is equated with the home where the child vies with his siblings for the parents' attention. Teachers see jealousy of children toward each other in their friendships. Two good friends may become jealous of each other when another child comes along, making a triangle.

Most of these situations work themselves out, but occasionally the jealousy becomes so strong that the child's school work and his social adjustment are jeopardized. A child who feels accepted and who becomes an active participant in a good school program is helped to overcome his feelings of jealousy, of not being wanted, or of not getting his share of adult and peer recognition.

A teacher who is aware of children's emotional needs can spot the jealous children and help them most by making them feel necessary and valued. When a child does not feel left out by the teacher or the class, his jealousy becomes minimized and his energy is released for learning.

Only occasionally does jealousy become extreme. If a child is not learning or cannot form good peer relations, the teacher should refer him for psychological study and assistance. If such service is not available, the teacher and the parent working together may be able to give enough help to make a real change in the child's adjustment.

SUMMARY

The particular symptoms discussed briefly in this chapter were selected because they are frequently noted by teachers and cause them concern. Ability to understand their meanings will enable teachers to be more successful in helping children and parents. These symptoms are of concern to parents, also, for the latter often look to teachers for understanding and suggestions for helping their children.

14

The Exceptional Child

The exceptional child is designated here as one who has some physical or mental characteristic which makes it necessary for the teacher to think about him in a special way. This designation includes the exceptionally bright or exceptionally dull child, the child with severe vision or hearing defects, the crippled child, and the cerebral palsied. There is a considerable body of material on exceptional children, and it is not the intent of this brief chapter to give detailed information in regard to them. Here, we shall give a point of view and discuss briefly the teacher's role in meeting the emotional needs of these children.

An exceptional child—like any child—has to be seen, first of all, as an individual with certain personality characteristics that have developed through interpersonal living with others. These living experiences have largely determined his attitude toward himself and his special ability or handicap. In other words, the exceptional child is, first, a child and, secondly, a person with a special ability or handicap. Attitudes and personality characteristics vary as much among these children as among others. A teacher should see this child first as any child, then try to evaluate the degree of special ability or handicap. This evaluation is essential if the school is to provide the right amount and kind of special attention needed. The teacher will want the assistance of specialists in making this evaluation— the physician, the psychologist, and individuals trained to understand these specialized needs or traits.

The exceptional child's mental health needs will be the same for him as for other children, but it may be more difficult for the teacher to help meet these needs. A cardinal principle for the latter to follow with a handicapped child is to accept him as he is. If the teacher can do this, he will help the child accept himself as he is and not want so much to be different.

The next important principle is for the teacher to refrain from making the handicapped child feel sorry for himself and to not show pity for him. He should help him become as self-reliant as possible. All exceptional children should be encouraged to be as creative and independent as possible.

The teacher has an important function in locating the exceptional child in his classroom and in helping others understand him. The mentally retarded child can be located only through a careful psychological and medical examination. So many factors contribute to a low score on a group intelligence test that it must never be used to diagnose mental retardation. A child may function in a manner that causes the teacher to suspect he is mentally retarded, but he may be an emotionally disturbed child who is actually very bright. The school psychologist can assist the teacher by giving a psychological examination and then recommending to the parents further study by a physician, neurologist, or psychiatrist. Following the complete study, a proper program can be planned to help the child.

If a child tests below 50 I.Q. on an individual examination, he needs very special training which most schools are not equipped to give. Usually these children are excluded from school; many are placed in institutions where they can receive special training. Some states are beginning to experiment with a school program in trying to meet the needs of this group. More experimentation is needed to show whether this kind of program is satisfactory. If it is found that children with such low intelligence can be kept at home with a training program provided in the public schools, then it will be essential for communities to set up sheltered workshops for them as they grow older. They will never be able to work without careful supervision, and they will be able to perform only very limited tasks.

If a child has an intellectual ability of 50 to 75 I.Q., as measured by an individual intelligence test, he requires special instruction in a class adapted to his needs. This special class program should be one in which the child can progress from the primary grades through high school, with some type of work experience at the upper level to equip him for work in the community when he is old enough to work. Children with this level of intelligence vary in their ability to learn certain trades or work, but many of them can become self-supporting in unskilled labor under supervision.

The crippled child in the classroom has a readily observed handicap. The teacher can be guided as to how much independence he can manage by observing him and by getting an opinion from the school physician. Many crippled children can be much more independent than parents and teachers think. The teacher will be doing them a great service by encouraging them to make the fullest use of their powers.

There are all degrees of cerebral palsy, from mild to severe. The very severe cases do not reach public school but are cared for in special schools or classes suited to their needs. The child suffering from mild cerebral palsy can usually function quite normally in the regular classroom. Some of these children who show only mild physical effects, however, have a complicating factor in the form of an emotional disturbance resulting from the brain damage which caused the condition originally. Some of these children are physically able to be with others in a normal classroom, but are so disturbed emotionally that it is impossible to keep them in a normal group. They are hyperactive, noisy, restless, irritable, and often aggressive. They need to be excluded from the normal group and have special provisions made for them in keeping with the policies of the school system. The teacher must call for help from the principal and the psychologist in arriving at the best plan for these disturbed, brain-damaged children. Considerable research is now being carried on in regard to cerebral palsied children, and we may gradually learn better ways of educating them.

The partially deaf or partially sighted child generally can function quite well in the regular classroom if the teacher is aware of his limitations and plans accordingly. For example, the hard-of-hearing child should be seated near the teacher when he is giving directions, and the teacher selected to work with the child should be one who enunciates clearly. The degree of deafness must be evaluated by the otologist, who will make necessary recommendations to the parents; the latter can then transmit instructions to the teacher and the school nurse. The partially sighted child should be seated near the blackboard and should have a special desk that will bring his written material nearer to his eyes if this is necessary. Most ophthalmologists feel that larger print is not essential for the partially sighted child and recommend that he use the same books as other children.

We find today totally blind and deaf children being brought into the regular classroom. Usually, the deaf child receives speech training in a special school before entering a regular class. When he has learned to read lips and to speak, he enters a normal class while continuing to receive special speech training. This instruction may be provided by the parents on a private basis or through a county or state rehabilitation service. The teacher needs to know what special help can be provided for the deaf child. The principal of necessity would be involved in the decision as to whether or not the school could accept a child with such a severe handicap.

When a blind child is placed in a regular classroom, he receives instruction in reading by a visiting braille teacher, provided as a rule through the county or state rehabilitation board. Since the child needs books for classroom use, braille material is supplied through the same county agency. The braille teacher comes to the school regularly to teach the child to read and brings instructional material.

Teachers are quite naturally apprehensive about having the responsibility of a blind child in the room, but the few who have tried it say that they find it a rewarding experience for themselves and for their group of children. It is amazing to see how independent the blind can be. Only further experimentation will prove whether or not it is wise to try to meet the needs of blind children in the normal classroom.

THE EXCEPTIONALLY BRIGHT CHILD

Many teachers need to rely upon classroom observation or

a group intelligence test to locate the exceptionally bright child. Although these methods are not the best, they can be helpful. The child who always finishes his work quickly and accurately and has an excellent vocabulary and a rich fund of information may be an exceptionally bright child. But so, also, may be the youngster who hates details, and who, therefore, fails to finish routine tasks on time because of boredom.

A child who scores an I.Q. of 130 or more on a group intelligence test is certainly superior, but is he exceptional? He surely has the ability to go as far as he wishes in higher education and can be successful in any profession. But, unless he has the interest and the motivation, he may do no more in school than the pupil with a much lower I.Q. score.

The pupil who scores below 130 or 120 I.Q. on a group intelligence test may be just as bright as the one who achieves that score, but he may be penalized by poor reading ability or an emotional disturbance. This is why it is difficult for the teacher to locate the bright child without the aid of an individual psychological evaluation.

If the teacher locates children who test 130 I.Q. or more on a group test, however, he should make an effort to provide a wealth of material for them to use and should attempt to lead them on to be creative and productive. These children should be encouraged to achieve at higher standards than the average students, but this can be done only if they are eager to learn and explore the wider horizons the teacher can open to them.

The teacher has a great responsibility in relation to these brighter pupils. They can easily become bored with school life and may fail to understand and develop their good intellectual potential. It is the teacher's role to help them understand and achieve. The bright pupil whose intellectual needs are not being met may easily become a "behavior problem" because his energies and intellectual abilities are not being put to creative and challenging use. Or, he may come to dislike school if he finds the curriculum dull and boring. His emotional needs are certainly not being met when he becomes bored and frustrated by the lack of challenging classroom experiences. He is not having the satisfaction that comes from a feeling of accomplishment.

In schools where there is a high percentage of bright pupils, proper attention and a challenging curriculum are usually given. In public schools where the bright pupil is the exception, the exceptional student can easily become lost in the crowd unless the teacher is alert to his potential and needs.

Comparatively few pupils test above 150 I.Q. on an individual intelligence test; it is questionable whether their needs—intellectual and thus emotional—are met in the average public school curriculum. Much attention is being given to the best ways to meet the needs of these children who are at the upper level of intellectual ability. The teacher who is interested in knowing more about this subject should consult some of the current literature on the subject. Should these very exceptional children be accelerated? Should they be placed in special classes with a special curriculum? Should they remain with their own age mates and have an enriched curriculum? These are the questions that need answering as we strive to meet the needs of these particular children.

SUMMARY

It is well to keep in mind that children are helped to achieve good mental health when they gain satisfaction in keeping with their interests and abilities. If this is true for most children, it is even more true for the exceptional children mentioned in this brief chapter. They need the teacher's special awareness and assistance together with the help of any specialists available in the school.

Part Three

How the teacher works with parents and the school psychologist

15

Helping Children through Parent Conferences

The teacher who is concerned with meeting the emotional needs of his pupils knows that he can be most effective in helping children if he and the pupils' parents can work together. Working together means more than telling a parent that things are going well or not going well for the pupil. It means that parents and teachers must sit down together as partners and try to plan ways for providing the best possible program for the child.

In many elementary

schools today, as well as some junior high schools, teachers hold regular conferences with parents to report on pupil progress. With this procedure all children—not just those with special adjustment problems—receive the benefit of thinking and help from these two very important influences in their lives.

The parent sees the child in a different environment than that in which the teacher sees him, and vice versa. For example, the parent sees the child in the close, intimate home environment where he has developed a certain status and a certain pattern of reaction. The teacher sees the child in a larger, more impersonal environment and in the peer society in which he will have to live and work. Sometimes the two pictures are quite different. To completely understand the child, each adult needs to get the rounded picture by talking to the other.

The child does not leave behind him the effects of the home influences when he comes to school; neither does he shed the influence of the school when he returns home.

Children are not machines; they are human beings with strong emotional feelings about themselves and others. These feelings are the result of experiences with others—first the family, then people in the community. Through these experiences the child has developed a self-concept that directly affects his learning in school and his ability to live harmoniously with others.

The child depends upon his parents and teachers to help him develop a healthy self-concept. If the parents and teachers are to fulfill this responsibility, they need to know each other and to work and plan together in the child's interest. This kind of planning is possible only through face-to-face contacts in the nature of a conference. The conference must be carefully planned by the school and the teacher. The school must plan adequate time for teachers to hold conferences, while the teacher must gather information and data about the child in preparation for her talk with the parents. The teacher gathers data from several sources, such as the cumulative record folder, observation of the child in the total school environment, test scores, the child's daily achievement, and occasional anecdotal records.

In all conferences, the teacher must keep in mind his purpose, although he may change his aims as the conference progresses if this seems wise. For example, a teacher who plans to report on a pupil's progress may decide against this procedure if a parent comes in upset about some of the child's behavior. In this case, the teacher would do well to listen to the parent's concern, try to help him make plans to help the youngster, and arrange a conference to report on pupil progress at a later date.

Conferences are held for various purposes: reporting pupil progress, obtaining helpful information about the child, and discussing a child's learning or adjustment problem while obtaining the parent's interest and assistance in working it out. Most parents want to gain certain things from a conference with the teacher. "How is my child doing in his school work?" "Is he liked and accepted by his peers?" "How does he get along with others?" "Is he popular?" "Does his teacher appreciate him?" (That is, does he like him, and is he aware of the child's abilities?) "Does he need help of any kind, and, if so, what?" Some parents want to know how the child stands in comparison to his group academically, but many are satisfied with information in regard to his personal growth.

Most teachers hope to gain certain objectives in a conference with parents. They want to give a thoughtful evaluation of pupil progress in terms of the individual, including his total adjustment. They want to get a picture of the child in the home as the parent sees him. They want to gain the parent's understanding and support of the school program. They want to plan with the parent the best possible program for the child, and to seek ways to help him if necessary.

The teacher should be responsible for opening the conference and for guiding its direction. How he does this will determine the success of the conference. While there is no one way to open any conference, there are certain techniques that will ensure smooth running.

If the conference is for getting acquainted and for gathering helpful information, the teacher should state clearly that this is its purpose. He can tell the parent that this is not a reporting conference, but that they will spend the time in talking about the child. The teacher can start by telling some of his observations or by asking a leading question. Usually, if the teacher tells of some interesting observation he has made or shows a bit of the child's creative work, the parent is easily drawn into the conversation. The teacher then guides the discussion so as to obtain pertinent information about the child's health, play activities, fears, hobbies, reactions to brothers and sisters, etc.

It is of utmost importance for the teacher to gain an idea of the child's psychological position in his home. Do his parents accept him or are they dissatisfied with him? Do they seem to favor other brothers or sisters? Do they seem to over-protect him? Do they provide all the supervision and guidance a child his age needs? All of these facts will help the teacher understand the child and his ways of responding to the teacher and to other children in the class. Usually this kind of information can be gained without the teacher's asking direct questions if he is alert to the importance of gaining it.

When the conference is to be a reporting one, the teacher should set the stage by stating that he will tell the parent some things about the child and encouraging him to ask questions if something is not clear. The teacher owes it to the parent to give a thoughtful evaluation of the pupil's total progress and adjustment. Parents tend to ask questions about the child's academic achievement, but are just as interested in social and emotional development. It is the teacher's responsibility to introduce this aspect of development. Parents usually are not very sure just what the school may feel are the important facts, and they look to the teacher for the lead.

When a child is not making a good adjustment in learning or in social growth, the conference is more than a report; it becomes also an exploration and a planning. This can be the most difficult type of conference to hold. There are certain techniques that will help such a conference be successful.

It is necessary to accomplish certain things in the first conference with the parents. It is essential to have them feel that the teacher is interested in the child, likes him, and wishes the aid of the parent in helping the child. If this much is achieved in the first conference, then teacher and parents can work together in the child's interests.

Since all people are different, there is no single way to achieve these goals. The teacher will have to feel his way by observing the parent's reactions. He can help the parent realize his interest in the child by having some of the youngster's good work available to show, by recounting some positive behavior that he has observed, or by describing some of the things he has done to help the pupil. He can then tell the parent that he needs his assistance—since two heads are better than one—and point out that the parent knows much more about the child than he does.

It is useless to gloss over the child's problems, unless the parent is physically or emotionally ill and cannot face them. Problems can be stated in a way, however, that will not antagonize the parent. If the parent senses concern rather than anger or annoyance, he will more easily accept the teacher's evaluation.

In this first conference, parent and teacher should try to arrive at some tentative reasons for the child's problems and lay a possible course of action. The teacher should tell what he plans to do in school and let the parent tell him what he plans to do at home. In other words, each partner should do his own thinking with the teacher guiding the discussion. If the child has a serious problem, the parent and teacher might decide to call upon the school psychologist for help in getting reasons for the poor adjustment—learning or emotional. Tentative reasons established and tentative plans made, the teacher should give the parent another appointment in the near future so they can compare notes on how things are going for the child and make other plans if necessary.

Very frequently, the parent will try to place the blame for a youngster's problems on the school. For example, if the child is not learning, the parent may say that this is the result of poor teaching. The teacher must then point out that all the other children in the child's class have learned normally. He should further state that some children do have trouble learning and that their job is to try to find out the reasons and then plan accordingly.

It is natural for parents to become defensive when a child has an adjustment or learning problem. It is natural for them to blame the school. Teachers would do well, however, not to become defensive. They should quietly state that they can understand the parent's feelings, but that the reasons for any given behavior are complex and no one factor can account for it. It is probably not any one person's fault, and their job is not to place blame but to make plans for helping the child. The help given any child will depend upon the nature of his problems and their seriousness. Many times, parents and teachers together can give all the help that is needed by understanding the child's needs and working together. Other times, it is necessary to call upon specialists in the school or the community for adequate assistance.

In an ideal conference, the purpose for which it was held

has been achieved and the teacher has been able to establish a feeling of true partnership with the parent. Each participant should genuinely feel that the other is concerned with the success and happiness of the child. The teacher should feel that he has gained information that will enable him to work more fruitfully with the child. The parent should feel that he better understands the school and the program that is being planned for his child. If the conference was a reporting one, the parent should feel he has gained a more complete evaluation of the child than he could gain from a report card or a written letter. He has gained qualitative information that is important to know. For example, it is not enough to know that the child is learning; it is also important to know whether the child learns with zest or only under duress.

It is important to know that the child gets along well with others, but also important are the kinds of relationships he forms. Does he reach out to others or does he wait for them to come to him? Is he a follower or a leader? Does he need help in making social contacts? If the conference was a problem-solving one, the parent and teacher should feel they have laid the ground-work for cooperative collaboration and that the way is open for more conferences.

The ideal conference is a "two-way street"; it is one in which both parent and teacher contribute, with the parent feeling completely free to ask questions. Teachers use a vocabulary that is clear to them but not to parents. Unless the teacher is careful of his words or makes the parent feel free to question, many statements may be misunderstood. To make the conference a "two-way street" requires time. The conference cannot be rushed through in fifteen or twenty minutes with the teacher doing all the talking.

The ideal conference is also one in which there are no "dead-ends." A "dead-end" is just what it sounds like. The teacher tells the parent that the child is not learning or that he is not getting along well with others. Then the conference ends. There is really little use in telling parents these things unless the teacher goes on to explore and plan. Parents do not know how to solve these problems alone; they look to the school and the teacher for guidance. If the teacher goes up a "dead-end" and stops, he is assuming that the parent can do something about these things. The parent has the right to an honest evaluation of the child's progress and adjustment, but this is not enough. Alone, the parent cannot make the child learn, nor can he make him get along better with others. A conference with a "dead-end" is no better than a report card that gives failing marks and shrugs off any further responsibility. The teacher and the school are failing to fulfill their functions when this happens.

One of the greatest blocks to teachers' and parents' working together is the strength of their own needs and defenses. Each partner has a job to protect. The parent needs to feel he is a good parent and has not failed the child; likewise, the teacher needs to feel he is a good teacher and has not failed the child. The parent has vested interests in the child as a parent; the teacher has vested interests in the child as a teacher. Each wants to feel he knows how to help the child. Because these are strong needs, anything that threatens them will cause the individual's defenses to arise. These defenses can block honest listening to the other person and hinder planning for the child. When one is busy defending himself, he makes no progress. The teacher must be aware of this danger in working with parents, and he must be able to help the parent maintain his parental status. The teacher must be aware of his own defenses and not let them make him react to the parent with hostility or resentment.

In all conferences between parents and teachers, the child

should feel that these two important people are his friends. He must not feel that they are "tattling" on him or telling about his "bad" behavior. If there is a problem and the child is aware of it, he should know that these two friends are going to talk about ways to help him. The older elementary school child might even suggest to the teacher certain things he thinks might be of help. The teacher must be sure, however, that the problem is one over which the child can exercise some control and judgment. Many times, a child cannot change his behavior until an alteration has been made in his environment to make him feel more acceptable and adequate as a person.

Certainly, with children in the junior and senior high schools who are busy gaining independence from parents, conferences must be held only with the knowledge and the cooperative planning of the pupil. If it is a reporting conference, the pupil should help evaluate and understand the reason for his marks. If he is failing, he should have a hand in trying to decide what is best to help him. Sometimes this requires guidance and advice from the school psychologist. The pupil should understand this and also know how the psychologist will work with him. If emotionally disturbed, he is probably unable to make constructive suggestions and the planning for him will need to be done by the guidance counselor, the psychologist, and the parents.

SPECIFIC PROBLEMS IN CONFERRING WITH PARENTS

Teachers repeatedly run into similar problems and have the same perplexing questions arise whenever they hold conferences. In this section, some of these will be discussed. The answers are hardly definitive, but they may be helpful to others in thinking through similar questions.

How do you get working parents to come for a conference?

Teachers and schools have tried different methods. Some parents can come for an early appointment before going to work if they plan in advance. Of course, this means that the teacher, too, must come to school early. Some working parents can leave work early and arrive at school around 3:30 or 4:00 o'clock for an appointment. Some schools give teachers the afternoon off and let them hold evening appointments for working parents. This relieves the teacher from putting in overtime in communities where many parents work; the teacher gives evenings in return for free afternoons.

How do you get an uninterested parent to come for a conference? Sometimes the "uninterested" parent is not really uninterested. She may have several other children at home and cannot get a baby sitter. She may not be well and find it hard to get out. She may have a sick husband or an invalid mother or father in the home to care for. She may be afraid to come to see the teacher because she fears authority or is afraid of what she may learn about her child. This parent seems uninterested because she gives excuse after excuse to keep from making an appointment or makes one and then does not come. It is necessary to try to find out why it is so hard for the parent to make or keep an appointment and to help her work it out. Some teachers offer to go to the home to see the parent, but this is not always satisfactory. There may be many interruptions in the home, and it may be impossible to talk in privacy.

Some teachers find that by being very friendly over the telephone and by sending home encouraging notes with the child, an "uninterested" parent will finally make an appointment and keep it. If the child's behavior is very disturbing or if he is not learning, it may be wise for the principal to insist on the parents' coming to school to discuss things and help make plans. The authority of the school must sometimes be drawn upon.

What does the teacher do with the parent who says that the child does not show the same behavior at home that the teacher is describing? It is important here to keep in mind the purpose of describing such behavior. Usually the teacher is concerned about the child, and her purpose is to gain the parent's understanding and assistance. It may well be that the parent does not see the same behavior at home or is just denying it. Whatever the reason, the teacher should say that children do show different behavior in different situations, and not argue the point. If the parent sees that the teacher is going to accept his statement and move on to discuss the school situation, he will be less likely to become defensive about it and feel he must defend his statement. The important thing the teacher must achieve is to get the parent to see a picture of the child's school behavior and realize that it is not desirable. They can then move on to planning.

How can a teacher handle a parent's criticism of another teacher? A parent who is defensive about his child and who is also afraid because he is having difficulty may try to see the cause as the fault of another or several teachers. It is well not to listen to such criticism if it can be stopped. The teacher can say that it is his opinion that these teachers are capable or that he is in no position to discuss them since he has never seen them teach. It is also well to state that it is not helpful to try to place the blame for the child's problems, but rather to see what can be done to assist him.

Should I.Q. scores or achievement test scores be given to parents? It is generally accepted by school people that I.Q. scores should not be given to parents because it is difficult to interpret them. It is also possible that the child will achieve one I.Q. score on an individual test and another on a group test. A parent can be given the general information that his child has good intelligence or that his ability is adequate for him to go on to college if he should ask for the I.Q. scores. If a child is not learning, a parent always worries for fear the child lacks ability. Then, he should be reassured if the school has a record of an intelligence test. He can be told that the child has adequate or good intelligence and that the learning disability is due to some other factor, if this is true.

Schools vary in their practices in regard to giving out achievement test scores. It seems to me that it is best not to give those out either because so many factors enter into the child's achieving a good or poor score. The scores are used by teachers, together with the pupil's daily work, to estimate his learning. The teacher sees the scores in perspective, but parents see them in isolation. Therefore, it seems best to merely state that the child did well, above average, or poorly if the question arises.

How can the teacher discourage attempts by the parents to help the child with homework if such attempts are seen to be harmful? There is nothing inherently harmful in a parent's helping a child with homework. Most teachers, however, want the child to do the work himself so they can see what the pupil is able to understand and achieve. The harm seems to come when the parent, dissatisfied with the pupil's school work, uses homework as a tutoring situation in an effort to help the child learn and achieve better marks. Parents often become very upset at a child's mistakes, and their anxiety is transmitted to the child who in turn becomes unhappy and defensive. When tutoring by the parent produces a combative and unhappy situation, it is better that it be discontinued. The teacher can attempt to get the parent to cease his efforts by saying that he will give the child the necessary help, by pointing out that the parent has been trying to tutor over a period of time without being successful, and by suggesting that it is now time to try something else. The teacher can also help the parent realize that the child finds it very difficult to expose his ignorance to his mother or father. He wants, most of all, to have his parent's approval, and it makes him very unhappy to have his parent see how much he does not know. The parent will want to think he can help in some way, and he may find it easier to give up the teaching or coaching if the teacher tells him that he can help more by doing things with the child that they enjoy doing together. A parent's friendship and warm companionship are the very best of help.

How can the teacher tell the parent that his child is mentally retarded? In answering this question, we will first assume that an adequate diagnosis has been made of mental retardation. The examination should include a complete psychological, neurological, and physical examination. When there is no doubt about the diagnosis, the teacher should probably not be the person to tell the parent this news; this responsibility is the school psychologist's or the examining physician's. Parents find it extremely difficult to accept this information and usually continue looking for other specialists to prove that the first ones are wrong.

If there is no school psychologist, perhaps the principal must tell the parent that the child will need a special program of instruction. Of course, some schools still do not have special classes for mentally retarded children; in this case, the parent must be told that the child will be given the best help available in the regular classroom but that he will not be expected to achieve like a normal child.

How should the teacher discuss the fact that the child may be retained in a grade another year? The whole question of retention is tied in so closely with a given school's philosophy that this is difficult to answer. Those who argue for retention believe that by repeating a grade a child will learn better or "catch up." Most studies made on retention refute this premise. Since children who have normal intelligence and good physical health are able to learn if they attend school regularly, it is obvious that the ones who do not learn are using non-learning as a neurotic way of life. Retention in a grade does not solve their problems.

A high school pupil who does not work cannot realistically be promoted, for he will see the promotion as inconsistent and incomprehensible. But we must not see retention as the solution to any pupil's learning problems (see the chapter on learning disabilities). Too often, a pupil repeats a grade and his failure at the same time.

If the school decides that a pupil must repeat a grade, he and the parent will have to be told by the teacher and the principal that the decision has been made because it seems best. It is to be hoped, however, that the school will make some attempt to get at the reasons for the non-learning and provide adequate assistance to the child. Repeating a grade is never an adequate solution.

SUMMARY

To hold a successful conference teachers need not know "all the answers." In fact, the best conferences are ones in which the teacher is able to get the parent to look at his child with greater understanding and to enlist his aid when there is need for joint effort and planning. Through this joint collaboration, the two partners can explore and seek answers to the child's needs. The teacher, as one trained in understanding child behavior, can guide the parent's thinking and the course of the conference. But unless the parent is motivated to do some constructive, critical thinking, the conference is not effective. The mere giving of advice is not successful in working changes in parental attitudes and practices. Parent conferences, if thoughtfully planned, are one of the educator's strongest tools in aiding pupils' emotional adjustment.

16

The Teacher and the Psychologist Work Together

As the preceding chapters have indicated, the teacher in the school—like the parent at home—has the major responsibility for the children under his care. Teachers give daily direction to their children. In most instances, the teacher is able to provide adequate assistance. But in every group there will be at least one to three children who have rather specialized adjustment problems, and the teacher will want to call upon the school psychologist for assistance.

155

General use of psychologists in the schools is just beginning to become the rule rather than the exception. Because of this fact, most teachers are not aware of what services the psychologist can give to them in their guidance of children. This chapter will describe what a psychologist can do to help the teacher.

In order to be of the greatest help, the psychologist should not be required to spread his services too thinly. While there are no definitive figures available at present, it is safe to say that no psychologist should be expected to service more than one thousand pupils—this is a high figure rather than a low one. With this ratio or a lower one, the teacher should be able to call upon the psychologist for help with children who are not learning well or not making good social or emotional adjustment.

Most schools that have the services of a psychologist provide a method of referral so that the teacher can communicate his desire for help with a particular child. A referral blank is provided for the teacher to fill out, after a conference with the principal as to the desirability of requesting study for the child. The blank calls for a statement of the child's problem as seen by the teacher, recent scores from group intelligence or achievement tests, a statement of physical well-being as given on the child's school health record, some evaluation of the child's relationship to his peers, his scholastic ability as rated by his teacher, a statement as to the child's length of time in the present school, and whether or not he has ever repeated a grade. This blank is quickly and easily filled out by the teacher who signs it and has it co-signed by the principal. It is important for the principal to know which children are being referred for study and assistance.

The teacher usually has the responsibility of seeing the child's parent before requesting a detailed study. The teacher suggests to the parent in a conference that it would be helpful to seek the assistance and advice of the psychologist. The parent's consent, cooperation, and understanding are essential. Some parents prefer to seek such help and advice from a private specialist, and should have the right to do so. When this is done, the parent will often report such advice as he receives to the teacher. More frequently, the school psychologist serves as a liaison between the outside specialist and the teacher.

When the parent has given his consent for a study through the school, the teacher fills out the referral blank and sends it to the psychologist. In the junior and senior high schools where there is a staff of guidance counselors, it is usually the counselor who is responsible for sending through the referral request to the psychologist. The homeroom teacher makes known the child's problems to the counselor, who proceeds to contact the parent for his consent.

When the psychologist receives the request for assistance, he usually talks first to the teacher or counselor to get a first-hand report about the child. Following this, he makes an appointment with the child's parents and gets a more detailed picture from them. He asks their reasons for being concerned about the child and explains the way in which he will work. Thus, the parent will understand and accept the child's report of his sessions with the psychologist at home. The psychologist explains to the parent that he will be notified as soon as the study is completed so they can discuss findings and recommendations.

The psychologist will use a number of diagnostic techniques in making his study, such as a variety of tests, interviews, diagnostic play sessions, and observations of the child in the classroom. The child's physical health is always ascertained through consultation with the parents. A physical examination will be advised if one has not been done recently and always if there are any physical symptoms present.

Following the completion of the study, findings will be discussed with the child's parents and recommendations will be made to help him. The recommendation may be therapy for the child, together with counseling for one or both parents. Just as the child needs help, so do the parents in knowing how to work with the child at home. In some schools, the psychologist provides therapy for the child if he has the proper training to do so. He refers to outside sources the child who is too disturbed to be treated in a school setting or who needs long and intensive therapy.

If the child's parents decide to use an outside source for the child's treatment, the psychologist may serve as liaison between the school and the therapist. In this way, helpful suggestions can be given to the teacher who is working with the child in the classroom. Following a study, the psychologist always discusses helpful procedures with the child's teacher. He maintains contact with the teacher to check on the child's progress after a plan of assistance has been established and determines whether further assistance is needed.

It is not always necessary to recommend therapy for the child. Frequently, the psychologist can make suggestions to the parents and the teachers which enable them to give the child sufficient help to overcome his adjustment problems, whether learning or emotional. Sometimes the child can be helped in a learning problem by a sympathetic tutor; the psychologist may assist in locating such a tutor. When this is done, the psychologist keeps in touch with the tutor to check on the child's progress. Some schools provide remedial reading teachers who work with children screened by the psychologist.

Frequently, teachers do not think it essential to refer a child for study but wish to talk to the psychologist about him. This is another useful service the psychologist can give. The teacher and the psychologist can think of ways to provide helpful experiences for the youngster, thus forestalling serious difficulties from arising. Sometimes, after talking about a certain child, it may seem wise to get the parent to accept a referral for study. This, then, will be the teacher's next step.

Occasionally, when planning a difficult conference with a parent, the teacher can call upon the psychologist for suggestions in planning the meeting and for ways to approach the parent.

Sometimes a child needs to have a flexible program worked out for him until he receives enough help through therapy to be able to go along with the regular program. In these instances, the psychologist can be instrumental in helping the teacher plan this program by using all school facilities, such as the art studio, shop, and library. In junior and senior high school, the psychologist can be called upon to help decide whether the pupil is capable of mastering the regular program or will need a modified one. Evaluating the pupil's potentials, he makes recommendations for an adjusted program when this seems essential or beneficial.

On a school-wide basis, the psychologist can locate the mentally retarded children who need a special class program and the gifted children who need greater challenge and intellectual stimulation. Usually, it is not considered essential to gain the parent's consent to administer an individual intelligence test. Such testing is a routine part of school procedure.

Case conferences—which include all of the school staff who come in contact with a pupil needing special help or assistance —can be planned by the psychologist who then explains in a general way the pupil's difficulties and discusses methods by which teachers who come in contact with him can help. In a case conference the teachers can also give the psychologist a clearer picture of the pupil's behavior as seen by them; their opinions help the psychologist make his diagnosis and recommendations.

In some schools the teachers and principals like to feel free to call upon the psychologist to assist them with P.T.A. meetings or parent discussion groups. Psychologists are usually glad to render this additional service when the meetings offer them an opportunity to contribute. The psychologist—like all other school personnel—has to measure the amount of time and energy available and plan his schedule to help meet efficiently the needs of his particular school.

If the school psychologist has a background in child development, as well as clinical psychology, and has also a knowledge of school curriculum and policies, he can assist teachers when they work in committees concerned with a good over-all program for children. He can also be of great help in planning the school-wide testing program. He is familiar with good group intelligence and achievement tests, and, while it is debatable whether or not he should give time to administer such tests, he can serve the school-wide testing committee in an advisory capacity.

SUMMARY

As this brief discussion shows, it is the teacher who has the prerogative and the responsibility of calling upon the psychologist for help in meeting the specialized needs of pupils. Most psychologists do not have the time to spend hours in each classroom observing children and deciding which ones should be examined, and it is questionable whether this practice would be desirable if time were available. Such a procedure might arouse anxiety on the part of both teachers and parents and get in the way of their exercising good judgment in living and working with children. Probably, most teachers prefer to assume the responsibility for requesting assistance when they see the need.

As teachers and psychologists have more experience in working together, they discover more ways in which the psychologist can be of help. The psychologist should be seen as a specialist in child behavior and should be called upon whenever the teacher wants an expert opinion or wishes to reinforce his own.

17

School Cooperation with Community Resources

Restricted by the very nature of its organization and functions, the school cannot meet all the special needs of every pupil. It is generally agreed that the prime function of the school is to educate—to teach the child the necessary skills, tools, attitudes, knowledge, and social adeptness that will enable him to live successfully in our society and to be a force for good in his community. This point of view suggests that the school will be concerned with any factor that interferes with its efforts to

162

achieve this end. Anything which hinders the achievement of these ends could be considered the concern of the schools. But there are other responsible agents in a community, too, and the school needs the aid of these agencies. Parents have rights and responsibilities in relation to their children, and these prerogatives should not be interfered with. The schools should be concerned with any factor that prohibits their doing a good job of education, but in certain instances they should call upon individuals and agencies in the community to help them.

Each community varies in the services available for its residents. The school must find out for itself just what these agencies are. The school nurse, physician, psychologist, or social worker can inventory these agencies for the school and refer to them when the need arises.

Let us suppose that a child is unable to learn because his actual physical needs for food and clothing are not being met. Usually, each community or county has some type of welfare service that can be called upon to give the family financial aid. The school nurse or social worker is the logical individual to counsel the family on seeking such assistance. Requests for this aid must come through the family to the welfare agency, but the school can advise the parent on how to proceed. In most counties and cities, families can obtain medical or dental aid for children when this is needed. Lack of proper physical and dental care may very well interfere with the child's success in school and should not be overlooked. The teacher, who sees the children daily, can discuss such apparent needs with the school nurse or physician who, in turn, can help obtain proper assistance.

In some communities there are special rehabilitation facilities available for the cerebral palsied, the blind, the deaf, and the crippled. Here again, the school nurse or social worker can be instrumental in seeing that children with such handicaps receive attention. The teacher's responsibility, if he becomes aware of such children through parent conferences, can be to direct the parent to the appropriate school authority for assistance. Severely mentally retarded children often come to the attention of the teacher through talks with parents. Any of these children can be called to the attention of the school psychologist who can then arrange for testing and help the parent seek proper assistance if the child is too retarded to enter school. Sometimes a teacher is the first one to learn of such a retarded child at home and, although having no actual responsibility in this situation, he can render a service by alerting the parents to their problem.

The psychologist is the school representative who becomes acquainted through the teacher with the child suffering a severe emotional illness. It is the psychologist's task to evaluate the degree of disturbance and to recommend the child be excluded from school if his presence is harmful to others or if he gains nothing from school attendance. The psychologist helps the family seek aid from community facilities, such as child guidance clinics and hospitals.

Sometimes the psychologist finds a seriously disturbed child who cannot be helped until the mother, who contributes to the child's disturbance, can receive counseling or therapy. It is questionable if schools should provide prolonged counseling or therapy to parents; this might better be the responsibility of a community agency or private therapist. The school psychologist makes use of community resources in assisting the parent to secure the needed help. A child guidance clinic or family case work agency supplies treatment for both child and parent. The school serves its function in educating the child by helping the parent obtain the needed assistance.

Provided the emotional problems are of a nature that will

respond quickly to help, it seems quite proper for schools to offer psychological counseling or therapy when the child's emotional problems interfere with his learning and living constructively with his classmates. Schools long have offered speech and remedial reading assistance to enable children to be more successful in school. When a child has a problem that prevents him from learning, it seems quite reasonable for the school to offer assistance not available through any other source. Such action serves the same educational purpose as special help in speech and reading.

The psychologist must determine, then, whether a child's particular problem can be properly treated in the school or must be referred to outside agencies or private sources. The teacher's function is to call the disturbed child to the psychologist's attention; then the two of them can work together in planning proper assistance.

Upon entering a particular school, the teacher should acquaint himself with school policies in regard to handling special physical and emotional problems and be guided accordingly. In all cases, it is imperative that the teacher confer with the principal before taking any steps. The principal is the responsible head of the school and the one to whom parents and agencies go when contacted by the school. In schools where no provisions are made to help specialized problems through a nurse, social worker, or psychologist, the teacher assumes the responsibility of contacting outside agencies with the knowledge and support of the principal.

The following public agencies are listed as possible sources of assistance for a child or family with a special problem that cannot be met through the school:

Family Case-Work Agencies   Children's Court
Child Guidance Clinics   Church Social Case-Work
Family Welfare Bureaus   Services

Hospital Clinics
Public Health Departments
State Travelling Mental
  Health Clinics

County Mental Health Asso-
  ciations
The Red Cross
The Salvation Army

SUMMARY

The school has its job to do, and other community agencies have theirs. The school cannot and need not take on functions that are properly and adequately met by other community sources. In a well organized community, each social agency—including the school—cooperates with others in its work of serving parents and children and in meeting their needs.

18

Conclusion

The opinions included in this book are written with a conviction born of experience. Words, however, are often inadequate to convey ideas completely and accurately. Perhaps my purpose has been accomplished if readers are encouraged to take a new look at children. If this new look arises through disagreement over certain statements, that is all right, too. The most stultifying force in the educational process is the continuance of activities and attitudes through habit

167

without challenge by critical analysis and questioning, erasure of certain outworn attitudes, and addition of new attitudes and ideas.

I have tried to present certain concepts of child behavior to help those working and living with children understand them better. I have pointed out the importance of personal relationships in the learning process and in the emotional well-being of children. Experiences with other people are most important for children. Through others, children see themselves as valued and worthy of acceptance and respect; through others, they learn and become successful.

Teachers are among the most important people in children's lives. The good influence of an understanding teacher is immeasurable. In this book are described ways in which a teacher can provide emotional support for all children, and be most helpful to an emotionally upset child. It is often an understanding teacher who enables a child to look at himself with new eyes and perhaps see himself for the first time as a wanted and worthy member of society. I have tried to show that this understanding and acceptance is a necessary part of the educational process and determines whether or not a child will learn. While teaching methods are important, personal relationships in the classroom are even more significant. Learning cannot be divorced from good interpersonal relationships and sound mental health.

Schools foster mental health when they provide a program in which children gain satisfaction from realizing their intellectual, creative, and emotional needs. Realization of these needs comes through the understanding teacher. We end, as we began, with the premise that good education involves more than teaching: it is the *more than teaching* that enables children's emotional needs to be met and makes a teacher's task infinitely rewarding.

SUGGESTED READINGS

Almy, Milly, *Child Development*. New York: Henry Holt & Co., 1955.

Davis, Allison and Robert J. Havighurst, *Father of the Man*. Boston: Houghton Mifflin Co., 1947.

Driscoll, Gertrude P., *Child Guidance in the Classroom*. New York: Bureau of Publications, Teachers College, Columbia University, 1955.

Farnham, Marynia L. F., *The Adolescent*. New York: Harper & Brothers, 1951.

Jenkins, Gladys Gardner, *et al.*, *These Are Your Children*, expanded edition. Chicago: Scott, Foresman & Co., 1953.

Jersild, Arthur T., *In Search of Self*. New York: Horace Mann-Lincoln Institute of School Experimentation, Teachers College, Columbia University, 1952.

Langdon, Grace and Irving W. Stout, *Teacher—Parent Interviews*. Englewood Cliffs, N. J.: Prentice-Hall, 1954.

Redl, Fritz and William W. Wattenberg, *Mental Hygiene in Teaching*. New York: Harcourt, Brace & Co., 1951.

Index

Index

K

Kindergarten children and school phobia, 86-89

L

Langdon, Grace, 169
Learning disabilities, 90-102
    case histories of, 98-101
    diagnosis of, 91-94
    in high school pupils, 97
    medical examination for, 93
    reasons for, 94-95
    teachers and, 96-98
Letter-substitution (see "Baby-talk")

M

Mental health:
    and controls, 25-26
    and pre-adolescent experiences, 27
    and school, 24
    and self-confidence, 9
    and the classroom, 3-36
    practices, 13
Mental Hygiene in Teaching, 169
Motivation, 92

N

Nervousness, 129-130
    causes of, 129
    teacher's role in, 130

P

Parent and school psychologist, 156-157
Parent-teacher conferences, 141-154
    problems of, 149-154
P.T.A., 160
Parents as aid to teachers, 10
Peer acceptance in the pre-adolescent, 27
    culture, 24
    identification, 22, 29
        in adolescents, 33
    relationships, 14-15
Praise, 7
Pre-adolescents, emotional needs of, 21-29
Problems of teacher-parent conferences, 149-154
Psychological counseling, 165

Psychologist, school (see School)
Public health departments, 166

R

Rebellion:
    and stuttering, 111-112
    and the pre-adolescent, 22
Red Cross, The, 166
Redl, Fritz, 169
Rejection:
    and school phobia, 84
    and withdrawing behavior, 76
Repeating a grade, 154
Resentment and stuttering, 111-112

S

Salvation Army, The, 166
Schizophrenia:
    and stuttering, 119
    and withdrawing behavior, 75-76
School-community cooperation, 162-166
School:
    and emotional needs, 6-7
    and mental health, 24
    guidance counselor, 33
    nurse, 163-164
    prime function of, 162-163
    principal, 165
    psychological counseling, 165
    social worker, 163-164
    speech specialist, 120
    therapy, 165
School phobia, 82-89
    and kindergarten children, 86-89
    reasons for, 83
    treatment for, 86
School psychologist, 33, 41, 68
    and case conferences, 159
    and learning disabilities, 94, 96
    and P.T.A. meetings, 160
    and speech defects, 120
    and truancy, 109
    assistance of, in obtaining community aid, 164
    decisions as to child's treatment, 165
    ratio to pupils, 156
    role of, 157-159, 160
    —teacher relationship, 155-161
    techniques used, 157

DATE DUE

DEC 1 2 '72	DEC 12 '72		
NOV 1 8 74	NOV 14 '74		
GAYLORD			PRINTED IN U.S A.